# NORWAY

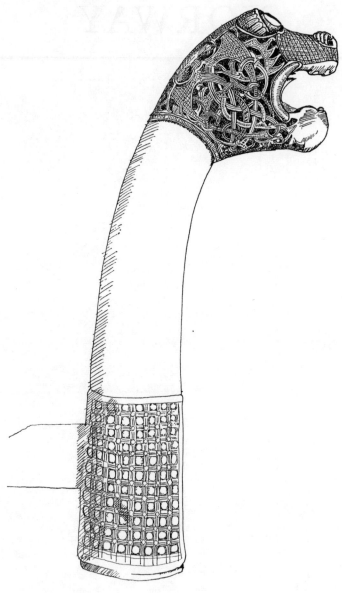

*Animal head post from the Oseberg Ship*

# NORWAY

Philip Caraman

*Illustrated by Lita Anker*

LONGMANS

LONGMANS, GREEN AND CO LTD
London and Harlow

*Associated companies, branches and representatives
throughout the world*

© Philip Caraman 1969

First published 1969

SBN   582   10798   9

Printed in Great Britain by
WESTERN PRINTING SERVICES LTD, BRISTOL

To
John W. Gran

# CONTENTS

# PREFACE

On the northern side of the town of Narvik there is a
large war cemetery where the combatants of several
nations are buried. When I visited it on Whit Monday
1966 I was looking for the grave of a fellow-Jesuit,
Père Xavier Rénom de la Baume, who as a young
lieutenant in the Chasseurs Alpines had been killed
in May 1940 in the retreat from Namsos. With little
trouble I found it below a cross just a few yards inside
the main entrance, and on the gravestone I put a pot of
azaleas to which I tied a note, written in Norwegian and
wrapped in cellophane to protect it from the weather.
It read: 'Lieutenant de la Baume, a Jesuit priest, gave
his life for the freedom of Norway at the time Jesuits
were proscribed by the Constitution of the country'.
I do not know whether anyone read it or how long the
azaleas remained over the tomb.

In 1956, fifteen years after de la Baume's death, the
Norwegian Constitution was revised for the last time
and the Jesuit Order to which he belonged became legal
in Norway. Nine years later, in 1965, when I came to
live in Oslo, a Jesuit was still a curiosity.

This was an advantage in writing a book on the
country. I began with impressions which I later checked
by reading. Although there is a standpoint that becomes
clear in the course of the book, it would be ridiculous
for any reader to assume that it gives a Jesuit or even a
Catholic view of the country—the first is a chimera, the
latter an absurdity.

My purpose has been to provide a traveller's companion, not in the manner of Baedeker (now re-edited
and indispensable) but in a more personal way that
nevertheless leaves out no essential information. During
three years in Norway I have visited nearly every part
of the country; on four occasions I have been in

# Preface

Trondheim, on three in Bodø. I have written about no place I have not seen myself.

The sources of the book are my own experience, my reading and conversation with persons of all classes, and a long journey from Oslo to the Norwegian-Russian border in the Arctic in the spring and summer of 1966. The last provides the framework of the book. I have tried to show the historical interest and associations of places, touch on questions not covered by the ordinary guide book and, more daringly, to answer the questions, what is life like in Norway? what kind of people are the Norwegians? The answers are my own and cannot be ascribed to those who have helped me with the book.

Among many friends to whom I am indebted for help I should like to mention John William Gran, Catholic Bishop of Oslo, at whose invitation I came to Norway, Atle Gadd Bjørkum, a Director of the Store Norske Spitsbergen Kulkompani A/s, who arranged my journey described in the last chapter, Herr and Fru Olav Henriksen, Dr Oskar Garstein, Fru Wenche Koren, Pastor Olav Waring; also Colonel Kristian Kristensen, who gave me introductions in the north of Norway, and Fru Lita Anker, who drew the illustrations for the book.

PHILIP CARAMAN

*Akersveien 5*
*Oslo*
*17 May 1968*

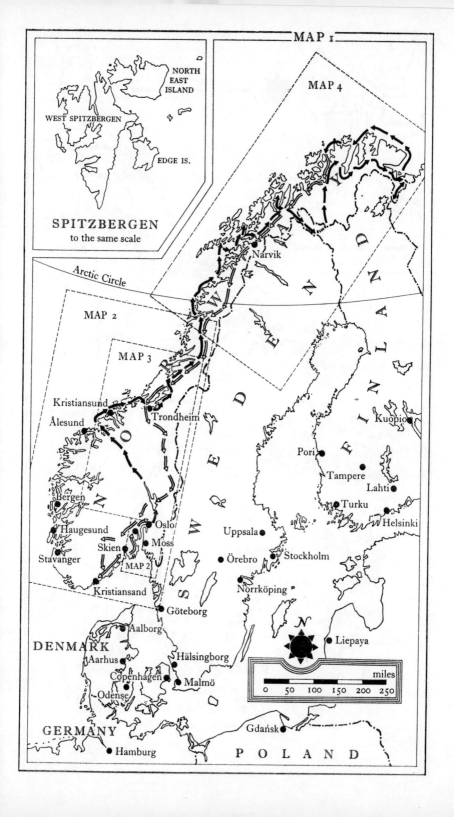

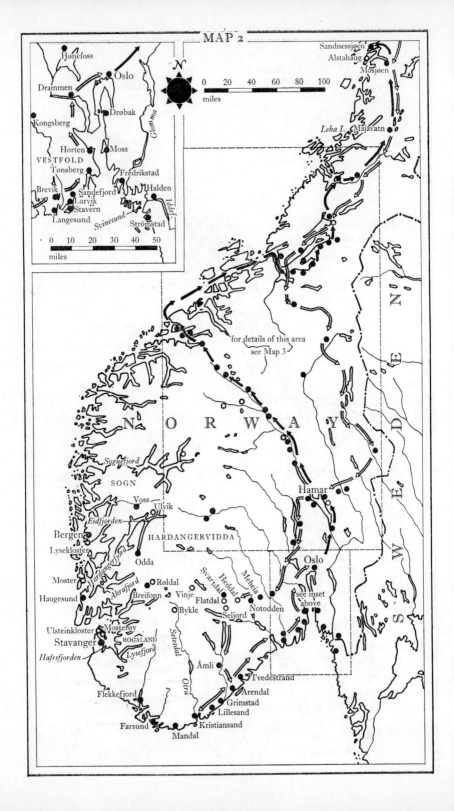

MAP 2

Hønefoss
Oslo
Drammen
Drøbak
Kongsberg
Horten    Moss
VESTFOLD
Tønsberg    Fredrikstad
Brevik    Sandefjord    Halden
Larvik    Stavern
Langesund    Svinesund    Strömstad

Glomma

Iddef

N

0    20    40    60    80    100
miles

0    10    20    30    40    50
miles

Sandnessjøen
Alstahaug    Mosjøen

Leka I.    Majavatn

for details of this area
see Map 3

N    O    R    W    A    Y

Sognefjord

SOGN

Voss    Ulvik

Eidfjorden

Bergen
Lysekloster
Moster
Haugesund
Ulsteinkloster    Mosterøy
Stavanger    ROGALAND
Hafrsfjorden    Lysefjord

Hardangerfjord    HARDANGERVIDDA

Odda

Røldal
Breifonn    Vinje
Bykle    Flatdal
Seljord

Svartdal    Heddal    Meheia
Hamar

Oslo

see inset
above

Notodden

Setesdal

Otra

Åmli

Tvedestrand
Arendal
Grimstad
Lillesand
Flekkefjord
Farsund    Kristiansand
Mandal

S    W    E    D    E    N

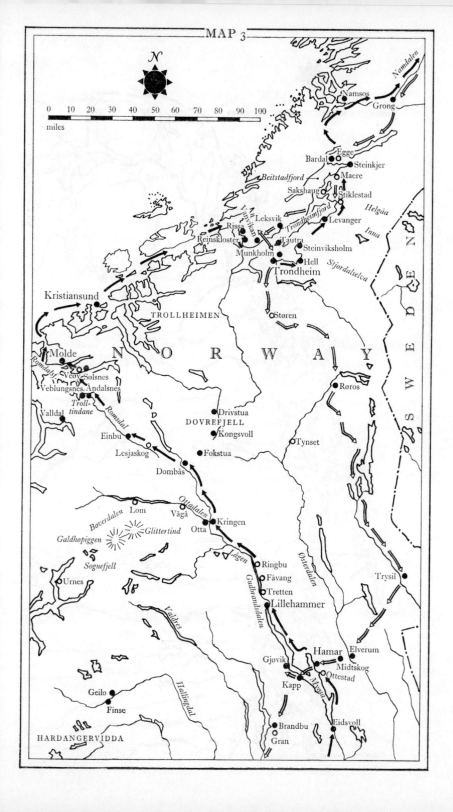

MAP 3

N

0  10  20  30  40  50  60  70  80  90  100
miles

Namdalen

Namsos
Grong

Bardal   Egge
Steinkjer
Beitstadfjord   Macre
Sakshaug   Stiklestad
Mt. Vardian   Leksvik   Levanger
Rissa   Trondheimfjord
Helgåa
Inna
Vanvikan
Reinskloster   Lautra   Steinviksholm
Munkholm   Hell   Stjordalselva
Trondheim

Kristiansund   Støren

TROLLHEIMEN

Røros

Molde   N   O   R   W   A   Y
Romsdal   Sveøy Solsnes
Veblungsnes Andalsnes
Troll-   Drivstua
Valldal   tindane   DOVREFJELL
Romsdal   Kongsvoll   Tynset
Einbu
Lesjaskog   Fokstua
Dombås

Bøverdalen   Lom   Ottadalen
Galdhøpiggen   Glittertind   Vågå
Otta   Kringen
Sognefjell
Urnes   Lågen   Ringbu   Østerdalen
Fåvang   Trysil
Gudbrandsdalen   Tretten
Lillehammer
Valdres
Hallingdal   Hamar   Elverum
Gjøvik   Midtskog
Kapp   Ottestad
Geilo
Finse   Brandbu   Eidsvoll
HARDANGERVIDDA   Gran

S   W   E   D   E   N

# MAP 4

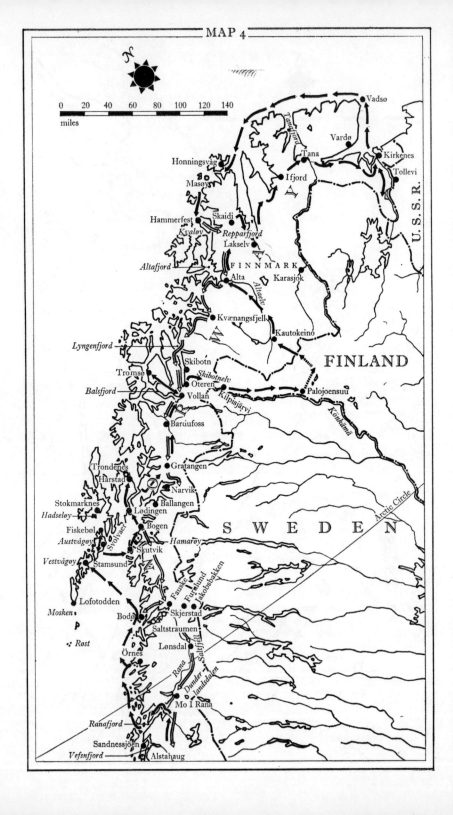

# CHAPTER 1
# OSLO

*Christiania, singular city, from which no man departs without carrying away traces of his sojourn there.*
                                    Knut Hamsun, *Sult*

*Christiania is the dullest capital in Europe—a day is quite enough there.*
        John R. Campbell, *How to See Norway* (1871)

After Reykjavik in Iceland, Christiania, now Oslo, is without question the ugliest capital in northern Europe. The modern section was built principally by German architects in the second half of the nineteenth century; most parts they left untouched were ruined by town planners in the period between the two world wars. Today a tourist can walk for hours on the unevenly-paved, characterless streets in the city centre without setting eyes on more than half a dozen buildings of pleasing façade or proportions. If it was the aim of the kings of Sweden, who were also kings of Norway from 1814 to 1905, to make certain that Oslo should never rival Stockholm in splendour, they succeeded. But they are not to blame. The fact is that Oslo, which was largely destroyed by fire in 1858 (there were earlier fires in 1686 and 1708) became the victim of the worst period of 'Victorian' and later modern architecture.

Norway in the nineteenth century was a poor country. Had the finance as well as the talent been available, Oslo today might be one of the finest cities in Europe. Its position as a capital is comparable to that of Istanbul. On a cloudless April day with the snow lying on the backdrop of fir-covered hills and over the small islands in the fjord, it has the appearance of a fairyland.

In any case Oslo is a reluctant capital. People live there under compulsion of work or circumstances,

I

seldom by choice. At heart they are country people, it can hardly be otherwise when in May, for instance, it is possible to ski in the hills in the morning and, the same afternoon, sail, swim or fish in the fjord. From the heart of the city it is only half an hour by electric train to the forests that are inside the city boundaries and as deserted as any area in the more remote countryside. At Christmas, Easter and Whitsun there is an almost total exodus of the population and Oslo then has the appearance of a derelict city; even the taxi driver goes out to the mountains or to his summer bungalow by the sea.

Somehow the architectural ugliness of the city matters less than it would in other places, for the surroundings compensate for it. From many humble

*Oslo harbour with the Town Hall and Akershus*

apartments in the suburbs the view over the city is superb. In fact, Oslo is best seen at a distance. From Holmenkollen or higher up, from Frognerseteren, it lies by a lovely stretch of water like a magical city; nearer, from Ekeberg, above the maritime school, all its architectural features can be picked out. Hovedøya, across the water from the town hall, is another good viewing point. But from all places it looks no more than an overgrown country town. No Norwegian would claim that it was a metropolis: it is the modest capital, unpretentious for the most part, diffident, only half-urbanised.

The Oslo resident is too honest to rave about the city; often he makes a joke of it. Yet it is a likeable capital, for it has few of the stresses of city life. The pace of its business is slow, a peace always descends on it at the week-end, there is no bustle at any time of the day or year, and although there is a rush-hour that begins at three-thirty, it is noticed only by the motorist. Outside the short summer tourist season, the city belongs to the citizens.

There are corners of Oslo, occasionally a row of houses, even a complete street, that give a hint of what it might have been had the Norwegians, not the Germans, rebuilt it after the 1858 fire: perhaps a grander Bergen or Trondheim, with enchanting painted timber houses and wharf-side emporiums in place of the present heavy commercial buildings.

From medieval times (the city was founded about 1050) only two buildings survive intact: the Gamle Aker (a replica of the old Catholic Cathedral of Oslo) at the top of Akersveien, a squat, beautifully proportioned, restored church, and the old castle of Akershus on a crag dominating the harbour: it is half-fortress, half-palace, a diminutive Tower of London that sits guard over the old city nestling behind it and epitomises its history. It was the seat of the Danish Governor of Norway; until recently there were houses in old Oslo with marks of cannon-balls shot from Akershus onto Swedish troops, who besieged it in three different wars, but for the rest there are only minute remains of the medieval city, unnoticed even by the native, a cellar here, some old arches, a derelict wall belonging to the palace of the medieval bishops, a friary or monastery.

From the wharf below Akershus, in both winter and summer, a ten-minute ferry crosses to Hovedøya, the largest island in the fjord, with its more substantial ruins of one of several Cistercian monasteries in Norway. The plan of the old buildings is easily traceable. James VI of Scotland (James I of England) went hunting here when he visited Oslo in 1589 for his marriage to Anne of Denmark: it was celebrated across the road

3

from the old cathedral of St Halvard, in Ladegården, formerly the Bishop's palace but then the residence of a rich citizen, Christen Mule. After the ceremony the King replied in Latin to the congratulatory speech of Jens Nilsen, Bishop of Oslo. When not engaged in festivities, the royal couple, passionate card-players, spent most of their time gambling. Today nothing remains of St Halvard's (it was closed and fell into ruins at the Reformation) and there are now plans for converting Hovedøya into an amusement park.

Apart from the modern cathedral, finished in 1679 and redecorated in fine taste after the last war, there is not much that survives from the period of Danish rule: it lasted from the Reformation to the Treaty of Kiel (1814) when Bernadotte, Napoleon's Marshal, was awarded the joint kingdom of Sweden and Norway for deserting his master in the moment of his defeat. Karl Johan, the hub of the city, is called after him. The present royal palace, with its Ionic portico, was built by him as a summer residence: a plain edifice finely sited in a park open to the public. With the exception of the University buildings there is little in Karl Johan of particular architectural merit. The Storting or Parliament building at the other end of the square presents what most visitors take to be its back, but in fact is its façade, to the royal palace. The State Theatre was an expression of the nationalistic movement, a moderately successful building in a Norwegian manner. In front of it stand appropriately the statues of two Norwegian dramatists of international fame: Bjørnstjerne Bjørnson, with his hands on his hips, and Henrik Ibsen, his arms behind his back in the fashion of an English royal personage. Hidden in the shrubbery on the other side is Ludvig Holberg, whose comic-dramas were written mostly for the Copenhagen theatre; in the formal garden between the parallel streets are some delightful sculptural groups, mostly children and deer, bordering on a pond. There is much Norwegian history to be learnt in the vicinity, for a statue in Karl Johan or the adjoining royal park is the equivalent of a monument in Westminster Abbey. Kristian Krogh, the nineteenth-century Norwegian painter, with a convex belly that retains the snow in winter months, sits growling at the Storting: it is a realistic sculpture accepted by the municipality after passing the pencil sketch now in the National Museum.

In his last years spent in Oslo, Henrik Ibsen walked most mornings down Karl Johan to hold court in the café of the Grand Hotel. He would be interviewed there by English journalists who assured him that in spite of Queen Victoria's disapproval of his work he would receive a warm welcome from London intellectuals; but he never visited England. Today all Oslo walks in Karl Johan. A military band plays at the palace end on Fridays, the Salvation Army has its meetings there on Sundays, old ladies eat their ice-cream cornets on the pavement, young couples neck under the trees and protest parades occur there. In summer more English than Norwegian is spoken by the afternoon crowds; in the evening tourists look out on what they take to be Norwegian life from the restaurants on both sides, Frascati, the Grand, the Continental. Blom, in an alleyway, between two bookshops, is the preserve of native artists, a prolific body in Norway; the *Norske Klub*, behind the Storting, is the most exclusive place in Oslo.

After the great fire of 1858 had destroyed the major part of old Oslo, the city was rebuilt between the Storting and the East Station on the American block system of intersecting streets. This is now the main shopping district, with small and specialised dealers as well as the large stores. Nearly every vista a brilliant city planner might have exploited is blocked by dismal buildings. Tramways add to the discomfort of a walk in a very compressed area.

Oslo reflects the nation; in that sense it is a genuine capital. Its change of name in 1924 from Christiania was a part of the same wave of civic self-assertion that produced its two most controversial embellishments—the Town Hall and the sculptures of Frogner Park.

The Town Hall dwarfs or dominates its surroundings with its two russet brick towers containing a carillon of thirty-eight bells. In the twenty years (1931–50) it took to build, every Norwegian artist then held in repute contributed to its decoration; the sculptors of the day adorned the approaches from the fjord and, more successfully, an astronomical clock was erected over the entrance on the city side. The Hall was a communal effort in every sense, a collective display of the talent of two decades, unique in Europe.

Frogner is more esoteric, the preposterous achievement of a single sculptor—acres of undraped statuary in every posture into which the human frame can conceivably be contorted, it offers a field-day for the student of the nude in stone or bronze: he can trace the increasing corpulence of the artist's models as he stuck without pleasure to his prodigious task. In winter the result is grotesque: for months icicles form long pendants to the naturally protuberant parts of his creations.

Gustav Vigeland, who was responsible for it, had genius matched only by the courage of the city corporation which commissioned him: the blame or credit must be shared between them. During the German occupation he was left undisturbed with his models and assistants behind a high fencing and a small percentage of the rates of Oslo was allotted to the execution of his stark vision. When the fencing was removed after his death, the people of Oslo were aghast. Vigeland's early work, clothed and almost classical in style—the statues of Niels Abel, the Norwegian mathematician, and the writer, Camilla Collet, both in the royal park, are examples—makes the choice understandable. But given a free hand his talent decayed and he became increasingly morbid. The central column that rises above the rest, a confused scrimmage of arms, breasts and bottoms, is said to represent a struggle for air and life: a research student has counted a hundred and twenty-one intertwined bodies between its base and apex. The tourist can interpret it as the nightmare of a madman groping tantalisingly for something beyond his grasp. With deliberate provocation Evelyn Waugh condemned it, and the whole park, as something more awful than the ruins of Hiroshima. It would be unjust to see a reflection of any national inhibition or exuberance in Vigeland's sick fantasy. More interesting than the park itself is the near-by Vigeland museum: it houses all his rejected ideas for the column and some of his early work, including half a dozen fine portrait busts.

Undoubtedly the same kind of groping afflicted the greatest of Norwegian painters, Edvard Munch. An entire museum, on the east side of Oslo, is devoted to his work: only there can his achievement be properly assessed, for comparatively few canvases of his can be found outside Norway, except in Germany, the United States and Sweden. He was obsessed with death, sex and himself. He died in 1943, a year after Vigeland. He is one of the few modern Norwegian painters who can stand comparison with the French impressionists: today his lithographs are among the most sought-after in the world. He is anguished, distraught, intense, yet in passages surprisingly tender. There are other paintings of his in the National Gallery, notably the much-reproduced *Girls on a Bridge*; his largest mural is in the main aula of the University building in Karl Johan; the wedding-room in the Town Hall is also his work.

The Norwegians, like other Scandinavians, have a talent for laying out a museum; this is particularly noticeable in museums devoted to a single subject, person or achievement. There are several at Bygdøy, the peninsula on the other side of the fjord from the Town Hall. Near the landing stage, in adjacent buildings, are the Kon-Tiki raft and Nansen's polar ship, the

*Fram*, and about a mile inland, the Viking museum. The lines of the Oseberg and Gokstad Viking ships are signally beautiful from every angle: the former is more perfectly preserved; it has a grand upsweeping prow decorated with a pattern of fabulous animals and is thought to have been a state barge rather than a sea-going vessel. With it were discovered in 1904 some animal head posts with interlaced ornaments and a ceremonial cart decorated on all sides with scenes from

*Carved wooden cart from Oseberg Ship*

Norwegian myths and legends. The Gokstad ship, unearthed earlier, is the larger of the two but less elaborate. In 1893 a replica of it, with gunwale holes for sixteen pairs of oars, was made, sailed across the Atlantic and exhibited in the Chicago World Fair.

In many by-ways of sport and adventure the Norwegians have established obscure records of endurance. The first and fastest man to cross the Atlantic in a rowing-boat was a Norwegian: he took fifty-five days in the year 1896. In 1836 Mensen Ehrat set up a still unbroken running record. It is said that in fifty-nine days he ran from Istanbul to Calcutta and back, averaging an improbable 94·2 miles a day.

Bygdøy also has its open-air museum similar in lay-out to those in Stockholm and Helsinki. With its stave church, turf-roofed houses, interior furnishings and decoration, farm and school buildings, barns and boat-houses, all authentic and scrupulously reconstructed, a tourist need go no further afield to get a valid conception of the Norwegian way of life from the twelfth to the eighteenth century. It should be seen in conjunction with the Historical Museum, in some ways the most interesting of all, situated behind the University.

There is nothing in Oslo corresponding to the Tivoli Park in Copenhagen. Formerly there was a central amusement place, the Klingenberg, which was demolished in 1930 to make way for the Town Hall: a cinema today commemorates the site. It had a theatre, a concert and variety hall (the predecessor of the *Chat Noir*) and restaurants. The most popular performer was an English acrobat, whose turn was followed by a Chinese knife-thrower and his fire-eating brother. A *camera obscura* and peep-shows attracted large crowds, but according to one English traveller the chief attraction was the merry-go-round, which held a 'higher social position here than in England: fathers, mothers, comfortable-looking middle-aged citizens sit seriously on wooden horses'. Balloon ascents were arranged over the fjord.

Nor has Oslo a Zoo. Norwegian law forbids the retention of wild animals in captivity, but off the road south to the Swedish border a park with deer, minks, lemmings and other animals has been fenced in: but as deer from the hills intrude into private gardens and elks occasionally come down into the city centre, no Norwegian bothers to visit it.

There is an unexpected contrast between the centre of Oslo and its suburbs—perhaps 'surrounding residential areas' would be a better description. Some of the most attractive domestic architecture anywhere can be seen on a visit to Bygdøy: large timbered mansions painted white and standing in well-kept gardens, they are reminiscent of New England yet intimately Norwegian. Here are the homes of rich shipping men, diplomats, the out-of-town residence of the King, modest, homely and, in fact, characteristic of the Norwegian monarchy. There are fine houses also in districts like Nordstrand, Holmenkollen, Smestad and nearer the centre in the roads to the east of Frogner Park. Unfortunately the urge to rebuild the city settles principally on the wrong areas. There is the danger always that many fine houses will be demolished on the plea that the ground on which they stand can be more economically used: it is argued, for instance, that space could be found for three thousand people in the Frogner area where there are now only seven hundred.

Rebuilding, however, proceeds slowly. Everywhere in Norway there are enterprises begun, abandoned or half-completed: a grand two-way thoroughfare peters out into a dirt road, years of discussion precede the addition of a single storey to an old museum. At the present pace the city will take two centuries to complete its face-lift. Sections between Karl Johan and the water-front, begun in the 'sixties, give promise of a fine modern idiom. Possibly, with all the rebuilding still to be done, a style will be developed, modern, native and worthy of Oslo's situation.

Curiously one of the first indications that this may happen is a private venture of the diminutive Catholic community. In the area of the Munch museum the central feature of a new housing scheme is a squat, square, fortress-like, red-brick building, which is the new Catholic parish church of the east end: the walls are blank and undecorated except on the side over-looking the harbour. Within the plain square encase-ment is a circular church with an inverted dome, a very original, possibly controversial, work of a young Norwegian architect, commissioned by the Franciscan Friars who have embedded in an interior wall a piece of masonry belonging to their medieval friary in Oslo. Surrounding it is a petal-like formation of high apartment buildings.

# CHAPTER 2
# PEOPLE

*The conformity [of Norwegians] is in its way exemplary.
Everyone keeps in line and stays in step.*
Henrik Ibsen to his mother-in-law,
3 December 1865

*The Church is the one thing that saves a man from the
degrading servitude of being a child of his own time.*
G. K. Chesterton, *The Common Man*

What is the native of Oslo like? A statue about fourteen
feet high in the corner of the market square in front of
the Opera presents him as a manual labourer, muscular
and starry-eyed, striding purposefully to his morning's
task. It is a theme that recurs in smaller dimensions in
country towns. A member of the Labour (*Arbeider*)
Party is an unattractive person in the flesh. Work is
something he shuns. He is happiest when he has a
sedentary job in the post office, filing unnecessary forms.
At pedestrian crossings he snakes his way through the
rush-hour traffic, asserting his right of precedence. His
hey-day comes at Christmas. Then, in the parcel
office or at the docks, he acts the little chieftain while
the sorely-tried citizen is shunted from counter to
counter until after half an hour his turn comes to
collect his Christmas parcel. The moment frequently
coincides with the official's lunch-time break. It is no
concern of his that the recipient's entire morning is
wasted.

The system, or absence of it, in the parcel post is
perhaps more primitive than in any European country.
The citizen collecting his goods endures worse irrita-
tions than a Russian bureaucracy could devise. Until
recently he was made to queue at the central post
office in order to pay a few pence on an understamped

11

letter. If he is sent goods by ship he may find himself unloading them from the hold, if by air he has to drive to the terminal to fetch a package that may not be worth the price of his petrol.

The men of the Labour Party as a general rule can be identified by their hard-used brief-cases. They can be seen with them principally on Saturdays and the vigil of holidays making their way to or from the *Vinmonopol*, the State-controlled liquor shops. Only here can wine, aquavit or whisky be had. (The quality is always good, often excellent, for the state buys on behalf of the whole nation and buys well.) No bottles are on display and the depots look more like banks, with frosted glass and curtained windows, as though they contained something evil to be kept from the gaze of children. It is almost a shameful thing to be seen in the precincts of a wine store: if an acquaintance is recognised in the same or a parallel queue, gazes are averted. On the eve of national holidays, police patrol the entrance. By law the customer must not emerge with a naked bottle; a ritual wrapping in brown paper takes place at the counter after the cash has been registered, and when several bottles are bought the assistants themselves place them in the brief-case. Only in Norway is a brief-case the essential possession of every adult male citizen, regardless of his degree of literacy.

In Oslo there is a state liquor shop in all the principal districts. With the exception of a handful of cities of the size of Bergen, there is only one in other large towns, none in the smaller places. A person living in the country may have to drive a hundred and fifty kilometres to purchase a bottle of table wine. Sometimes an air journey is necessary, as between Farsund and Kristiansand in southern Norway. If bottles are delivered by carrier it is the gossip of the entire hamlet.

Such restriction on the sale of liquor is inconceivable in Catholic countries. In northern climates it can be an incentive to drunkenness: its effectiveness in Norway as a means of curbing a national weakness is now debated. At drink parties every bottle that is opened must be finished. Youths purchase alcohol as soon as they are the age for it: in Finland they show their passport at the counter. Yet Norway is no worse than other Scandinavian nations. The drunk Norwegian is not normally aggressive; the Finn, man or woman, in the same condition, is liable to whip out his knife. The problem is most acute in the darkest days of winter, when it is not uncommon to meet drunkards in the street as early as ten a.m. and they can be seen collapsing in the gutter during a cloudburst or at night sometimes lying curled up in sleep against a mound of snow.

There is work in Norway for everyone except these *uteliggere* (literally, men who lie out). But among them there is a camaraderie not found in other groups of the population. In a club organised for them by the Franciscans in the east end of Oslo they will spend the evening over coffee and cakes telling stories against themselves. 'Long Tom' attends regularly. He managed for three weeks to keep a job as a scene-shifter at the Opera House until one night, when *Carmen* was being performed, he placed in the centre of the stage the nearest prop he could find, which happened to be the throne for the king in *Aida*. He was sacked but he appreciated that 'you could not have Egypt in the middle of Spain'. More pathetically his friend who eventually found work in a State hospital lost his job when he was discovered drinking the raw alcohol in which he was supposed to sterilise the surgical instruments.

These men have a horror of the winter when they may have to pass a shelterless night. If they enter private or public premises for protection, they fall foul of the law: formerly in Norway there was an officer in every town, the *stodkonge*, whose job it was to arrest wandering strangers and imprison them. Bjørn, another club member, was arrested in an Oslo museum. He had wandered in through a back door and happened to be looking out of a basement window when a policeman passed. He offered the explanation that he was there to clean the windows. Unfortunately it was a Sunday and he got two years.

All persons found drunk in the street or in any public place are liable to a fine of seventy-five kroner (about £4.10.0). The *uteliggere* seldom has so much and has to go to prison for some days or even weeks while other citizens get off comparatively lightly. All who are found at the wheel of a car (stationary or in motion) after exceeding the statutory limit of one glass of beer or wine are put in prison for twenty-one days.

While Norwegians on the whole take regulations lightly, they observe the drink laws with scrupulosity. At dinner parties one guest will often not drink in order to be free to drive others home; taxis, when they can be had, are the common solution. It is the supreme courtesy of a host to take thought of the way his guests will return home.

Prosecutions under the drink law are frequent, but the offender is free to choose the time he will serve his three-week sentence. At Christmas, Easter and summer there is a rush on the prisons. Face-saving is easiest at these times. A sympathetic friend will let it be known that the offender is out of town, if not on the Spanish riviera, then in his mountain hut or summer house on the south coast. The law makes no exceptions. There was an occasion when the leading brain surgeon in Oslo had to serve a period in gaol. He had no replacement and the people of Oslo with cerebral tumours could only wait patiently for his release. Norwegians can laugh at the absurdities of their own laws, which nevertheless remain unaltered on the statute book.

After the drunkard and the member of the Labour Party, the most easily recognised type is the Pentecostal Brother. He is as single-minded as the Fifth Monarchy man of Cromwellian England. There are clusters of them in Oslo, but the bulk of them is found in western Norway. Their religious adherence blends ill with the Norwegian character and brings out its worst traits. They are humourless, moralistic and lacking in charm. It is probably not accidental that their conventicles are often adjacent to private or public baths.

The war virtually eliminated the small Jewish community. Seventeen Jews are said to have returned in 1945. Many had lived in the same street, Rostedsgate, near Jakobskirke, on the east side of the river Aker. The entire street was emptied of its occupants, who were transported to Germany. There were others who with the help of the Norwegian underground organisation were shepherded safely into Sweden. The Jews, however, had never been numerous in Norway: today they are scarcely ever met outside the big cities.

The unaligned Norwegian, who forms the great bulk of the population, prides himself on his independence, which is often superficial. Certainly he does not take to drill. He is a good fighter when he has to fight, but he is not militaristic. The royal guard parades outside the palace but its movements have no precision or smartness; the uniforms are often unpressed, the boots unpolished. Marching with their rifles at the slope, they will scratch themselves behind the ear, stroke a child under the chin or wink at a girl friend. The moment they are off duty and out of uniform they are indistinguishable from other citizens. The martial type, the moustached colonel, or the fiery sergeant-major does not exist. However, it is improbable that the Norwegians, as the Swedes do, will accept conscripts with shoulder-length hair. There is a tradition of military profession in certain families, perhaps not as pronounced as with the clerics.

This contrasts with Finland, a military-minded nation nurtured in the German tradition. On entering a restaurant or café, the Finnish conscript sharply clicks his heels and salutes the proprietor, and he does the same on leaving. The Norwegian will slouch in with a cigarette in his mouth and an illustrated magazine under his arm.

Youth is very much in the foreground of Oslo life: it is to be expected in a country which has the finest sports facilities and camping grounds in Europe. But they are not a problem in the same way as in Sweden. They are not seen in drunken packs in the main streets; only in Halden on the southern border are the streets dangerous at night; and it is the Swedes who do the wrecking there, driving over the frontier bridge and turning the town into a rodeo circus. There are cafés in Oslo, particularly in Universitsgaten, where the youth gather by compulsion on Saturday night: they are mainly well conducted. Sport, especially in winter, gives them a healthy outlet for their high spirits. After an evening's skiing along illuminated forest tracks or

*Skater*

skating on lakes or the upper reaches of the fjord they fill the electric trains back to town, singing to the accompaniment of banjos, more sober and gay than they are likely to be after they have settled down to married life. They work hard, as they must do in a country that has only two universities.

At every age the great mass of the population keeps in step. The scandal that Ibsen caused in his day was that he struck against conformity; since his time conformity has become more widespread owing to the levelling process of taxation.

There are, of course, exceptions and eccentrics, but the great majority follow a set pattern of behaviour: they ski because others ski, they are Lutherans because it is the 'done' thing; there is monotony in the internal furnishings of a flat, in the food and the preparation of it, in recreations and reactions. Nonconformity is as uncommon in the kitchen as in the conscience. From the age of seven, when the Norwegian first goes to school, he learns to 'keep in line and stay in step'.

Yet, man for man, at the middle and lower income levels he is better educated than the Englishman. The tram conductor will read Ibsen, go to the ballet or enjoy the classical composers. The business man has many shelves of books in his home. English is well spoken by a large number. Many are familiar with English writing from Shakespeare to Ian Fleming.

The Norwegians themselves have many criticisms of their educational system, but its end-product is satisfactory. An egalitarian society produces competitiveness at an early age, and the Norwegian child in consequence takes its schooling seriously. Teachers have the advantage of holding a respected position in society; moreover, they are well paid, university educated, with a marked sense of vocation. Because schools end in the middle afternoon, many teachers follow a second profession in the long evenings; they are artists, writers or journalists.

The main obstacle to any improvement in Norwegian education is the chaotic state of the language. It is a hard-used joke that every Norwegian speaks four languages of which three are Norwegian. The facts fit the jest. Until 1870 Norwegians and Danes used the same speech, the same grammars and dictionaries. Ibsen's Norwegian is the Danish of his day: his language is known as *riksmål* (also called *bokmål*, for it is mainly used by writers); today it is the speech of the professional classes. But alongside the Danish speech there was the language of the country people that derived directly from medieval Norwegian. During the nationalistic movement in the nineteenth century it was systematised by Ivar Åsen and popularised by him in books that appealed to simple tastes; it is a synthetic tongue derived mainly from western dialects. From the 1850s this *nynorsk* (or *landsmål*) began to establish itself as a rival literary language. The confusion was increased in 1938 when an artificial blend of the two (*sammnorsk*) was propagated. It is the language in which the laws are written; today it has its fervent advocates, but most people see in its increasing use the doom of Norwegian culture. And with all this chaos there have been three major spelling reforms since 1905.

There is some sense in the suggestion that the problem should be solved by the adoption of English as the national speech. Children have organised themselves in processions to the Storting demanding that one Norwegian language should be taught in schools. Within the same family parents will speak *riksmål* and their children *landsmål*, which happens to be the language used in their classrooms. In the *Norske Theatre* Ibsen's plays, which can be understood by everyone in the original, are performed in translation into *nynorsk*. All three languages are used on the radio and television, as well as dialects, which often have much vigour and vividness: there is a valley in Oppland, for instance, where three different words are used to indicate a couple of persons, according to its composition as two men, two women or a man and a woman.

In a small country (and measured by population Norway with its close on four million must be reckoned

# People

small) divisions naturally run deep. It is a condition that produces in Oslo, a city smaller than Dublin, three times as many daily newspapers as New York: in addition every town and district of any size has its own daily paper; there are a hundred and sixty altogether. A journalist of mediocre talent has no difficulty in placing his articles. On the extreme left is *Dagbladet*, radical slanted, well edited and famed for its correspondence. The tourists should know that when in difficulties with state officials a threat to 'write to *Dagbladet*' is instantly effective. In England the equivalent would be a letter to his Member of Parliament.

From January to April, year after year, all the papers carry pages of reports of local and national ski competitions. Holmenkollen day (the ski jump there dominates

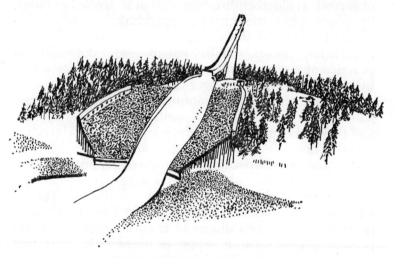

*Holmenkollen Ski-jump*

the surroundings of Oslo) marks the climax of the season.

*Aftenposten* is the most bulky, solidly established, widely read daily paper with a standing above the rest. It is characteristic that the principal morning paper should be called 'Evening Post': it surprises no one in a country where the political 'Left' is the Right Wing Party, 'free teaching' given for a substantial fee, *middag* (midday meal) taken in the evening, *nynorsk* or New Norwegian the old language; the guest arriving for dinner is greeted with 'good day'; the tourist in search of entertainment finds the 'autumn show' running in early summer.

The Norwegian is all the more attractive for his inconsistencies. He is an intuitive rather than a logical creature. He is well represented among the arts— music, literature, painting; he is too occupied with nature to have time for the abstract: the Norwegian philosopher is an unknown phenomenon. On the other hand he is infinitely curious about the daily life of his neighbours. 'The one thing dearest to his heart', observed a nineteenth-century visitor from Scotland, 'is gossip—not the rattling, sparkling, inventive, ill-natured gossip of the female tongues, but real, solid, inquisitive gossip.' With gossip goes the national practice of staring: both originate in the hamlets where little happens and a stranger is instantly noticed.

Norway was never conquered by the Romans, Christianity came to the country comparatively late and there were never any Norwegian Orders of Chivalry. This is not to say that the Norwegian is either un-chivalrous or unchristian in his behaviour, but only that the roots of his culture are Viking. In blood the Norwegians (with the exception of the natives of Bergen) are the most unmixed race in Europe: there is no trace of any inhabitants of their country before its present people, whose origin is guesswork. It is this that many Norwegians believe distinguishes their outlook from that of other nations. The same Scot, at the end of his tour of Norway, admired the 'hardy Norwegian, whose progenitors are also direct ancestors of us in these lands and, more especially of the lowland Scotch'; he was impressed by their gigantic frame and strength, but found them phlegmatic and lethargic: 'In him [the Norwegian] the sanguine temperament degenerates into the lymphatic. What he wants as a race is an infusion of Celtic blood, which would give him fire and dash, while retaining the substratum of physical powers and calmness of judgement.'

The Viking culture explains also the customs surrounding more festal meals. Today as in the time of Olav Haraldsson the banquet lasts all evening. It is punctuated with speeches by the principal guests, who rise often more than once. There are occasions when the company will sit down to table at eight o'clock and adjourn after midnight for coffee and liqueurs. The longest official banquet recorded in Norwegian history was given in Håkon's Hall in Bergen by Håkon IV in the thirteenth century: it lasted three days. Today, when a foreigner enters a restaurant he usually becomes impatient at the snail-like pace of the service; but no incivility is intended: the diner must appreciate that for the Norwegian the restaurant meal is an evening affair. If it takes three hours, that is not abnormal.

In a class of its own is the *Julebord* feast. From the beginning of December until the middle of January all the hotels and restaurants in Oslo advertise their *Julebord* or Christmas feasts. Down the length of the dining-room a long table is piled high with every conceivable kind of *hors d'œuvres*, meat, fowl, fish dish, and a seemingly endless assortment of fruit, dessert and cheeses. For an all-in price the diner can eat as much and as long as he pleases. He may start at six in the evening and end after midnight; if he is in a party he will dance between courses or sections of courses. At *Julebord* business parties I have watched a poor Chinese client of a Norwegian shipping magnate aghast at what was expected of him. Starting with an entire lobster, he blinked his slit eyes when he was invited to follow it with eel, oysters or herrings before setting out on the cold reindeer or roast beef, the last entrée before the serious part of the meal. Pig-ribs—customary Christmas fare—is an essential. The unpractised *Julebord* man can do no more than nibble at the cream cakes or cheeses. There is no Christmas pudding. If you present one to a Norwegian family, it is likely to be served with potatoes and vegetables.

From early December as many as fourteen pages of *Aftenposten* are devoted to *Julebord* advertisements. Danes come up on the night ferry from Copenhagen to join Oslo *Julebord* parties. The leading restaurants cater usually for as many foreign as native clients. The principal class distinction in Oslo is between those who can afford the *Julebord* and those who cannot.

The ordinary dinner party is more formal than in England but nevertheless relaxed. The foreign visitor should be prepared for a ceremonial beginning and close to the dinner itself. It is a social solecism for him to start drinking before his host has welcomed his guests in a short speech and raised his glass to *skål* them. At the close the principal guest will make a speech of thanks on behalf of his fellow-diners. As they all, men and ladies, leave the table together they file past their hostess, shake her hand and thank her for the meal. Coffee and cognac follow, frequently cakes, and towards the end of the evening, whisky. Before leaving the guests thank their hostess again for the evening, then thank each other for their company.

A resident in Norway should learn the more simple rules of *skål*ing. Beer and water are generally not regarded as *skål*ing liquids. At table, on the sacred word, all raise their glasses, and holding them at the ready, wait for the host to catch the eye of each guest in turn. Then they can drink; but the ritual is not over. The eye-catching is repeated with glass still in hand.

Pundits on the etiquette of *skål*ing give detailed, conflicting and subsidiary rules, seldom observed with precision, for the more private *skål*s between guests. It is well to keep some wine undrunk for the final *skål*

# People

proposed by the principal guest. When fowl is served, after the hostess has indicated her permission, it can be eaten in the fingers in its later stages.

In the eighteenth century the welcoming *skål* was accompanied by a song. An Englishman, E. D. Clarke, describes a dinner party he attended in Oslo in 1799. 'The master and the mistress of the house, rising from their seats, perform a brief recitative, as a preliminary song to the toast they are about to propose. In these solemn airs the whole company joined. . . . In this manner we drank *The Wooden Walls of Old England, British Commerce, Rule Britannia, God Save the King.*'

Letters of thanks are expected, and at their next meeting—even if it occurs six months later—the guest must remember to thank his host once more, *Takk for sist*—thanks for last time. Three or more years may elapse and friends meeting again will thank each other for a kindness received at their last meeting. *Takk i like måte*, is the reply—'Thank *you* also'. Before refilling his tank at his local petrol station, the motorist will thank the proprietor for his last service rendered.

Individually and as a nation, perhaps because of these conventions, the Norwegians do not fail in gratitude. An awareness of it permeates both domestic society and international relations.

In Scandinavia where the second person singular is a living usage as in France a distinction of value is created in personal relationships: the form *du* corresponds roughly with the French *tu*. It is used only when friends are on Christian-name terms. The moment is reached by agreement or chance, more commonly at the end of a convivial evening than in cold blood: otherwise the transition can be as embarrassing as a public marriage proposal. It is made always by a lady to a man, or by an elder to a junior, a superior to an inferior. The person honoured thanks the proposer and the two clasp hands. If it is accompanied by a *skål*, the parties link the arms in which they hold their glass while they drink each other's health. The unwary foreigner commits a blunder if he inadvertently slips back from the personal to the impersonal form. All children are addressed as *du* even by strangers and address grown-ups in the same way. Often persons who work together professionally use *du* accompanied by the surname, as for instance, *du Andersen;* it is a common half-way usage. Without artificiality *du* is used of God in the liturgy.

Close Norwegian friends have said to me that foreigners must learn to excuse them much because of their climate. Bernt Anker, the leading citizen of Oslo at the end of the eighteenth century, gave the same explanation to English visitors he entertained so lavishly at Frogner (his house is now the town museum): *huit mois d'hiver et quatre mois de mauvais temps.* The last words of the dying Osvald in Ibsen's *Ghosts* are 'The sun . . . the sun'. The largest mural of Edvard Munch (in the University Aula) is of the rising sun. The summer visitor, who often happens to enjoy warmer weather than in his own country, does not understand this; the resident does.

# CHAPTER 3
# BERGEN-STAVANGER

*Northward of us the people are too unpolished to*
*encourage the traveller to take a tour of the country.*
Erick Pontoppidan, Bishop of Bergen,
*The Natural History of Norway* (1775)

Bergen is more like the capital of another country than the second city of Norway. The Norwegian is alert to this but not the foreigner; the Norwegian will tell you that whether he approaches it by sea from Oslo (a three-day journey) or by rail (the time taken is the same as to Copenhagen) he has the sensation of entering another country: instinctively he finds himself looking for his passport and foreign currency. The Bergensere, as the people of Bergen are called, have a detached superiority of manners and speech. They regulate their life without reference to the capital. For them Bergen is Norway. When their young men travel abroad for the first time and are asked the country of their origin, they are instructed by their parents to reply, not Norway, but Bergen. In the reckoning of natives anyone not born in Bergen is to be pitied for his lifelong handicap. In their countryside they have a derogatory word, *stril*, found curiously also in Cork which for a hundred and fifty years was a Viking settlement: it designates the people, either from the mainland to the north or from the small islands to the west, who are disqualified from citizenship by their distance from the centre.

But with good reason the native of Bergen is a citizen of no mean city. Its site was chosen nine hundred years ago along an arm of land protected by seven mountains looking out into the world across the North Sea. Its foundation is recorded in the Snorre Saga: 'King Olav [Kyrri] founded a merchant town in Bergen, where very soon wealthy people settled

25

themselves, and it was regularly frequented by merchants from foreign lands.' It grew quickly and in the twelfth and thirteenth centuries was the capital of Norway and the largest city in Scandinavia. Today the medieval, the Hansa and the modern mercantile buildings blend against the mountain setting: King Håkon's Hall, the old Maria-kirke, the new hotels and the painted timbered ware-houses might always have been there. Somehow Bergen escaped the worst of the nineteenth-century architecture and understandably stirs the envy of the people of Oslo.

Until the twentieth century Bergen had only 50,000 inhabitants and, in spite of having no university, was the cultural capital of Norway. Ludvig Holberg, the eighteenth-century dramatist, Edvard Grieg, the musician (his house above a small lake just outside the city is a tourist attraction) and Ole Bull, the violinist and composer, were all natives of Bergen. Its summer music festival is one of the best known of Norwegian international events.

Like the old city of London, Bergen has its own trading customs, rules and traditions: a world within a world. From its foundation it looked outward towards England and the north coast of Europe. The reconstructed remains of Lysekloster, a Cistercian monastery

*Lysekloster near Bergen*

founded from Fountains in Yorkshire in the twelfth century, are a reminder of the close ecclesiastical ties between England and west Norway. The ruins stand a little back from the sea about fifteen miles south-east of Bergen.

The foundation was made by Bishop Sigurd of Bergen. After a visit to Fountains he brought back a small band of monks under the leadership of a Norwegian, Ranolv, who had been a Benedictine at St Mary's, York, before becoming a Cistercian and a founding Father of Fountains. This was in 1146. The next year Oslo followed Bergen's example. Hovedøya, on the island facing Akershus, was founded from Kirkstead in Lincolnshire. The first abbot is thought to have been a Norwegian who, like Ranolv, had joined the Cistercians in England. His name is recorded only in its Latin form, Adverus.

Traders followed the lead given by the monks. The first commercial treaty between the merchants of Bergen and England was signed in 1217.

The boat from Newcastle today takes twenty-four hours but in the last century travellers found the passage almost as frightening as an Atlantic crossing. For many English visitors who change here onto the coastal steamers for the much-advertised voyage to North Cape and the midnight sun, Bergen, their point of departure and return, remains their only memory of Norway when the rest is forgotten.

The tourist who does not visit the fish market and have a meal of boiled cod does not know Bergen.

The fish market, which is at the head of the quay at the centre of the city, is open every day. Fish in Bergen is stale if it is not alive the day it is eaten; fish two days old stinks. The native buyer surveys all the tanks which contain live fish, points to the fish he fancies, which is then netted and held up for his inspection. The fish is there and then killed, de-gutted, taken home and eaten for *middag*. Thus even the commonest fish is always savoury.

*Torsk* or cod is a delicacy in a class of its own. When it is fresh 'cooked' in the Norwegian manner, served with boiled potatoes and butter sauce, and its accessories (entrails, tongue, liver) laid out in a separate dish, cod becomes also a rite. Cod is the Christmas fare in Bergen. Few fish dishes are more tasty. Certainly Norwegian cod merits all the ritual that surrounds it, particularly when the Lofoten catch is flown down from Bodø in February.

There is no greater fool than the tourist who despises cod as the food of the working class: he must enter into the spirit of the meal and be unsurprised when the waiter proposes red wine to accompany it. That is usual, in fact right. In cod-eating clubs of Oslo it is taken also with aquavit chased down with beer. Bergen is the capital of cod in Norway south of Trondheim. All fish there is good: halibut by deft preparation becomes a greater luxury than salmon. The tourist who insists on meat in Norway will return to England with a grumble.

A rabidly anti-Catholic Scot after visiting Norway in the last century had only one good word for the Catholic Church: it fostered the Norwegian fishing industry. After labouring the obvious, that the people of Bergen and the Norwegian coast lived mostly by fishing, he evokes a picture of the appalling disaster that would strike Norway if the Pope relaxed the law of Friday abstinence from meat. There was ground for his apprehension, for even Elizabeth I, as head and governor of the Church of England, was compelled to reintroduce Friday abstinence in order to save the English fisheries. 'Millions upon millions of haddock and cod', wrote this traveller, William McTaggart, in 1887, 'are dried annually and exported to France, Italy, Spain, Portugal and even in large quantities to the far-off Brazils and South American Republics—in fact, all the Catholic countries where fasting on fish is enjoined one day in every seven.' An exhortation to fair-mindedness followed: "Think of this, O Protestants and iconoclasts.

# Bergen

Before you brace yourselves to the last great effort of
tearing Rome from the hearts of the people, the Scarlet
Lady from her chair, and the priests from their altars,
pause and reflect. I do not say that the downfall and
destruction of the Catholic religion should not be the
aim of all good people, but prior to action it should be
regarded from every point of view.'

From McTaggart's viewpoint the only benefits con-
ferred on Norway by Rome were to be measured in
exported cod. Norway grew fat on the abstinence of
the Scarlet Woman.

It is the gloom more than the darkness of the winter
in this part of Norway that depresses the visitor. There
is no compensation till the snows come. Leprosy
survived longer here than in other parts of continental
Europe. At Bergen, not far from the centre of the city,
was Norway's last surviving leper hospital. Here
Dr Armaner Hansen, a native of Bergen, discovered the
leprosy virus in the nineteenth century. Lepers from
Norway and other European countries were sent here
to be cured by him.

The climate in Bergen is mild and wet. It rains on the
average every other day, but when the sun shines views
can be had from Mount Ulriken across the islands
scattered over the sea approaches to the city. In the
summer there are flowers everywhere: in the streets,
gardens, houses and on the quay. The Norwegian makes
a religion of flowers. In winter a guest invited to dinner
perhaps for the second or third time is expected to bring
flowers for his hostess. In the smartest restaurants a
single carnation, rose or tulip costing as much as seven
shillings is set on every table. It gives comfort by remind-
ing the diner that spring is certain to come once more.

The short-period visitor to Bergen can, if he is well
instructed, learn a great deal about the culture of west
Norway without going far afield. There is no folk-
museum, but beyond King Håkon's Hall some of the
most valuable or historic houses of Bergen, removed

from newly rebuilt areas, have been reconstructed and furnished in period; also for the benefit of the tourist a stave church, removed from Fantoft in the Sogn district in the hinterland, has been reconstructed on a piece of high ground just twelve minutes by bus from the city centre.

It is the tragedy and charm of old Norwegian architecture that nearly all building was done in wood. Fire, rot and time have left little today. There are many medieval stone churches of great simplicity, particularly north of Trondheim, where English influence was strong; but the majority of medieval churches in Norway are, like Fantoft stave church, weird, square, pagoda-like structures native to the country yet at the same time strangely alien: their complex system of construction is peculiarly Norwegian, easily readaptable to pagan worship. It is as though the people, on their conversion to Christianity, built in a style that would be equally serviceable if they reverted to paganism. The Viking, like the Norwegian today, was reluctant to commit himself fully to Christianity.

The earliest churches date from the tenth century and were built by the same men who designed the long ships. Of more than two hundred that survived into the nineteenth century, just over twenty remain today, mostly in the western fjords and uplands. None exist in Trøndelag, though remains of them have been found there. Fantoft illustrates most of the common features of the stave church: the separate roofing of each section, the flying exterior dragons, the outside cloister, the bell-tower, the rack for worshippers' weapons and the lich-gate. At Lom, Urnes, Borgund and other places these churches stand on their original site and are more arresting: they stare out into the landscape like fierce primeval beasts, looking all ways, with a circle of protruding necks and fantastic threatening shapes, or perhaps like giant trolls about to rampage through an innocent and cowed countryside.

# Bergen

Mariakirke, off the quayside, with its twin towers rising above the old part of Bergen, is among the most interesting churches in Norway, one of three surviving from the thirty-three churches in the medieval city. It is little changed except for the seventeenth-century

*Borgund stave church*

addition of an ornate pulpit—an attractive and almost universal addition to the old churches of Norway. The altar piece is from Catholic times; the central wood carving of Our Lady flanked by the twelve apostles— Paul, not Matthias, doing service for Judas—is the work of German artists from Lübeck. The only considerable fragment of the old murals is a fine figure of the crucified Christ between two arches on the north side of the nave; other decorations show the influence of the towns forming the Hansa League, an organisation, in the days of city states, comparable to the European Common Market. There are names of German, Dutch and other foreign merchants on the eighteenth-century monuments in the graveyard.

Of all the old churches in Norway Mariakirke has best preserved its Catholic atmosphere. It is as though Bergen, cut off until the twentieth century by rail and road from other cities of Norway, retained more appreciation of the *res Catholica* that had moulded the outlook of its citizens. There could be nothing more totally Catholic and at the same time Norwegian than the thirteenth-century crowned statue of the Madonna at Austråt or from Urnes (the most perfect and untouched of all stave churches) now in the Bergen Museum: the refined features of the Westland peasant girl, her fair complexion, flaxen hair and transparent blue eyes are transferred to the Madonna. Today only the people of Bergen, among Norwegians, have some understanding of the position of Our Lady in the plan of the Redemption. It may not be altogether fanciful to ascribe to this residual devotion the more courteous, almost chivalrous, attitude of the Bergensere to women. Certainly a Catholic from the Continent feels more at home in Bergen than in other parts of Norway.

*Madonna and child,
Austråt chapel*

At the Reformation all but a few churches in Norway became anonymous, exchanging old dedications for a place-name. While today in England Norwegian influence can be traced through the churches called after St Olav—in London, York and East Anglia—the reverse process is impossible. Apart from one in Valdres how many Norwegian churches were dedicated to St Thomas of Canterbury? His death certainly made a deep impression both in Iceland and Norway. The legendary life of the saint was translated into Icelandic and widely circulated, and there are many allusions to him in the Icelandic sagas. The earliest representation of his murder is on a small brass shrine, once used as a reliquary, in the Valdres Church. It is known that pilgrims from Norway and England paid the reciprocal compliment of pilgrimages to Canterbury and Trondheim. The saga of Hrafru Sveinbjarnarson, the Icelander, tells the story of his catching a narwhale which he had difficulty in landing. He promised the whale's tusks to St Thomas if he would help. He did and the tusks adorned Thomas's tomb until the Reformation. Canterbury was seldom omitted from the itinerary of Norwegian pilgrims to the Holy Land until in the fourteenth century the route via the Netherlands was preferred.

Bergen is as good a place as any in Norway to study the process of the Reformation. It is a subject of which all but a handful of scholarly Norwegians are ignorant. Certainly it is agreed that it was put across deceitfully by a foreign power, namely Denmark, as a reform of the Roman Church, almost identical in nature to the recent revolution effected from within by the Second Vatican Council. The country people neither sought nor welcomed it. They were as conservative then as they are today.

The ecclesiastical section of the Bergen Museum illustrates the gradual character of the change: it is also a revelation of the grandeur of Norwegian medieval art. There would seem to have been Celtic influences as well as English: unquestionably the Vikings had a capacity for learning from the people they conquered and their contacts with Ireland survived their expulsion from Cork and Dublin. Certain motifs are curiously reminiscent of Byzantium.

While officially saints were ousted from the liturgy, they continued as the principal decoration of the country churches: the painted wooden altars and pews are mostly from the seventeenth century and the themes, colouring, technique and composition are in an unbroken tradition; the continental influences, mainly Flemish and German, are the same. There was no iconoclasm on a national scale as in England. There the building of elaborate mansions by the new nobility saved craftsmen from unemployment, but in Norway it was not until the eighteenth century that the old skills were diverted to domestic decoration: even the painted bedsteads, chests, stools and tables of that period show a striking continuity, the same soft greens, yellows, reds being laid on in streaks by the same peasant artists, floral designs slowly replacing figures. The finest examples come from the western valleys and Telemark.

From the time of Holberg the more famous Bergen-sere have made their name outside their own city. Edvard Grieg is an exception. His life-work was done in Bergen; he died there in 1907, surviving Henrik Ibsen by a year.

Grieg's great-grandfather was an Aberdeen merchant, Alexander Greig, who emigrated to Norway after the battle of Culloden and reversed the vowels of his family name. The countryside inspired Grieg's music: the long fjords, the sharp winds, the waterfalls and snow, the Hardanger district with its unique fiddle made and played there today (it has an extra set of strings which vibrate untouched below the regular set) and, further east, Jotenheimen, with its glacier: Grieg often climbed it, though for most of his life he had only one lung. 'I do not reflect', he once said, 'but write straight from the heart, whether the result comes out Norwegian or Chinese.' It never came out Chinese.

# Stavanger

Voss, Ulvik, Urnes and other places that get passing
mention in the smallest guidebook are part of Grieg's
world. His greatest friend was Rickard Nordraak, who
died at the age of twenty-four and is remembered for
composing what later became Norway's national
anthem: once he advised Grieg: 'Listen to the unclothed
plaintive melodies that wander like so many orphans
round the countryside. . . . Let them all tell their
stories.'

Bergen is the most convenient centre for excursions
into the western fjords either by road or steamer.
Sognefjord, the longest in Norway, to the north, and
Hardanger to the south, are the best known. Tourist
boats or regular ferries can be used; on a series of trips
the cumulative charge of taking a car abroad can be
considerable.

There is a hydrofoil as well as a ferry to Stavanger
calling at Haugesund on the way. Åkrafjord with its
steep banks is as magnificent as any in Norway.
Lysefjord, more easily visited from Stavanger, is
starker: for many people in Westland it is the grandest
fjord in all Norway. A third of the way from its mouth
a peculiar formation of rock, known as the *prekestol* or
pulpit, is a challenge to tourists: it is a two-hour climb
over rocks from the nearest point of the road but the
view from the summit is one of the finest in the world.
Across the entrance of the fjord leading into Stavanger
many islands are scattered, among them Mosterøy,
where the old Augustinian monastery, Ulstein Kloster,
has been rebuilt and furnished as a conference and rest
centre.

The Province of Rogaland, of which Stavanger is the
capital, is unlike other parts of Norway. The stone walls
on the hilly countryside recall the Lancashire fells; even
the mountain formations are unusual.

Stavanger itself has again a feeling utterly different
from Bergen. The old cathedral there, which many
prefer to Trondheim's, was dedicated by an English

Bishop to an English saint, St Swithun, Bishop of Winchester. Like Oslo's old cathedral, it is Romanesque. The finest section of the city lies above the quay on the

*Stavanger cathedral*

south side; there are unspoilt streets, parallel and crossing, of white-painted old-timbered houses rising in tiers to the ridge looking out on to its fine sea approaches.

Today Stavanger is the Mecca of sects; historically, it could be described also as the Plymouth of Norway. In 1821 Cleng Peerson from Tysvaer, a little north of Stavanger, and Knut Eide from the island of Fogn, sailed from here to investigate conditions for a possible colony in the United States. Three years later they returned with a favourable report. A sea-captain was hired and a small sloop *Restaurationen* purchased; with fifty-two men and women on board she sailed from Stavanger on 25 July 1825 and anchored at New York on 9 October. In November the colonists reached their destination, Kendall, then called Murray, in Orleans county, New York. There they bought land from John Fellows at five dollars an acre, agreeing to pay back the loan in ten yearly instalments.

# Stavanger

From Kendall a daughter settlement was made at Muskego in Wisconsin in 1834. In 1845 the first Norwegian paper, *Nordlyset*, was published in the States; the previous year the first Norwegian Lutheran Church had been founded.

Thousands followed, driven partly by the old Viking craving for adventure, partly by the failure of the potato crop, simultaneous with the Irish famine, in 1847. The American soil yielded richer returns for their labour.

Today there are more Norwegians in America than in Norway. As a body they were the best-educated immigrants. Farming was their most common pursuit. In rural districts they became more prosperous than other national groups. Socially they were more self-assertive, politically, for the most part, Republicans; in civic life they became serious politicians and, unlike the Irish, not opportunist. Inexplicably a stag rearing on its hind legs beside the lake below Stavanger Cathedral commemorates 'the men and women of Norwegian blood who contributed to the building of America'.

Today Bergen, not Stavanger, is the gateway to Norway for most Americans of Scandinavian origin on visits to unknown relatives; for English winter tourists it is the starting-point of their railway journey to the ski-resorts of Voss and Geilo. The Dutch business man bound for Oslo is a fool if, after flying to Bergen, he does not take the day train from there to Oslo; it is the grandest railtrack in Europe.

The journey lasts seven hours; the coaches are irreproachably clean, the food good (usually fresh fish with delicious sauces) and the seats adjustable: footrest, paper basket, refreshments, writing-table are available.

Like the Channel tunnel, the Bergen–Oslo line was discussed for a hundred years before construction began. It crosses wild country along the cliff side of fjords where no road can go, climbs to over four thousand feet near Finse (Captain Scott, observed by Amundsen,

practised here for his run to the South Pole), descends
to Geilo, a town of winter hotels, through Hallingdal to
Hønefoss and Oslo. In winter the track over the
mountain plateau cuts its way through walls of snow
sometimes twenty feet high.

It is the best way of seeing dramatic scenery from an
armchair. The Norwegians have built their railways
without disfiguring their countryside. An English
traveller remarked on this as early as 1876 when he went
from Trondheim south on the first section of the projected rail link with Oslo. 'Here I rode for the first time
in my life in an utterly unvandalising railway. I hope for
his soul's sake that Mr Ruskin will go to Trondheim
in order that he may travel on this line and thereby
become reconciled to engineers and pardon them
before he dies.'

# CHAPTER 4
# HAMAR

*I have never thought it necessary to drag about a*
*revolver, but nevertheless there are some freshmen to the*
*country who do so. When not exhibited as a threat it*
*becomes an absurdity, Norway to the stranger being a*
*much safer place than London by night.*
John R. Campbell, *How to See Norway* (1871)

Neither Oslo nor Bergen is typical Norway. There is
still the middle and north of the country. Most Norwegians know little more than the south; many have
travelled no further than Trondheim, very few further
north. And why should they?

Kirkenes, on the Arctic border with Russia, is
several hundred kilometres further from Halden on the
southern border with Sweden than Halden is from
Rome. In summer the roads are bad, in winter impassable. There is a mystery about the north for
Norwegians who have never visited it; and it holds a
magic for those who have.

Its mystery is less dense today than in the eleventh
century when Adam of Bremen wrote his description
of the people there. In these 'vast deserts and mountains
of snow live herds of monstrous men, who shut out all
approach; also Amazons, Baboons and Cyclops, having
but one eye in the middle of their foreheads; herman-
topedes, skipping or leaping with one foot only;
man-eaters without speech'.[1]

Until well into the present century the north could
be reached only by sea. Looking at the endless barren
mountain ranges from a few miles off the coast, a
medieval traveller might well believe that the kind of

[1] Adami Tractatus, *De situ Daniae et reliquarum Septentrionalium*
*Regionum* (1080).

people described by Adam of Bremen did in fact inhabit this region. 'Who can live there?', a fellow passenger asked me when I took a short hop on one of the north-going tourist boats.

Until the last quarter of the nineteenth century Norway was largely unknown to the rest of Europe: English writers of the time started their books on the country by explaining its geographical position. Then suddenly between the years 1880 and 1881 it attracted notice. 'The Prince of Wales [later Edward VII] and Mr Gladstone have both been there', explained one writer. That was all that was needed to make it fashionable. Nevertheless warnings were given against the danger of leprosy. In 1880 it was reckoned that there were still 2,000 lepers in Norway out of a population of two million.

A spate of travel guides followed, written mostly by English country gentlemen who described at length their feats with rod and gun. There were others who stepped ashore only at the ports visited by the packet boats from Bergen that sailed regularly to the North Cape. There was no adventure today in this method of seeing the country. I was determined to explore it by land. My first plan was to drive from Mandal at the south-west tip of Norway across the Arctic border near Kirkenes to Murmansk. *From Mandal to Murmansk* was a ready-tailored title for a travel journal: it contained the known and unknown, was alliterative, easy to remember and likely to last.

However, on 10 May 1966, I was compelled to leave Oslo before obtaining permission to cross the Russian-Norwegian border. The head of the Soviet section of the Norwegian Foreign Office advised me to delay my application until later in the year: perhaps the throng of tourists would then make the Russians open the frontier post. The principal travel agencies could do nothing for me. The previous summer a young American citizen had crossed into Russia in this area, perhaps inadvertently. Some months later he was reported to have taken his life in a Russian gaol.

A hundred years ago every tourist party on arriving in Oslo or Bergen hired a *tolk* or travelling interpreter who was often a costly bore: he expected his food, board and a *daler* (about 4s. 6d.) a day. Public transport was restricted to the fjord steamers, which in the early days of controlled sale of alcohol were used by natives as floating taverns. Along the principal roads a *carriole* could usually be hired. The driver sat very low in his seat, which rested on a long shaft and was placed between the horse and the axle. The shaft acted as a spring and the driver's legs were stretched forward to rest on a footboard so that if the horse stumbled he was not pitched out head first but brought to his feet standing on the footboard. Anyone who could not 'jolt in a cart, sup on porridge and sleep with a flea' was advised not to visit the country. On the rougher mountain tracks a horse was used. There were stages, usually at farm-houses ten to fifteen miles apart, where they were available.

Few Norwegians then spoke English and the Englishman who knew only the phrase, '*Straks, hest!*', 'A horse, instantly!', was a national joke. The *hest* was commonly the *fjording*, a straw-coloured, short horse, as sure-footed as the mule, usually good-tempered, that is seen today all over Norway. On the fjords private boats could be hired at prices scaled according to the number of oarsmen. Mr Bennet, described as 'a most useful Englishman who lives in Christiania', supplied a guidebook with all the laws of posting and boats, and an appendix of 'tables for calculating charges at a glance'. Mr Bennet's business has now developed into a travel service covering all Norway and other countries.

The people of Oslo are unstinting in their advice to friends. This year mid-May was barely the end of winter. Experienced drivers urged me to start out with winter tyres: I could abandon them at Trondheim.

Others claimed that they were unnecessary; some suggested chains in case I ran into ice on mountain passes. It was essential to criss-cross the windscreen of the car with adhesive tape as a protection against flying grit; in case of a breakdown in a desolate area it was prudent to subscribe to *Falken*, a national rescue service for motorists. Drivers, sleeping in their cars at night after a forced stoppage, had been found frozen to death the next morning. I was assured that this was not an unpleasant mode of expiry.

My predicament called for the protection of St Christopher, the patron of travellers. Every cradle Catholic finds himself in middle life with residual superstitions which he is reluctant to jettison. But there was no medallion of the saint to be bought in Oslo. The Catholic cathedral possessed a large relic of St Olav, Norway's patron, donated by the Catholic Queen of Sweden, Josephine, in the last century. While it might be a precaution to shave a splinter from the bone, I thought my journey scarcely warranted the sacrilege. I envied St Helena on her journey back from the Holy Land after locating the site of the crucifixion. Loaded with trophies of her travels, she found on unpacking in Rome that the bodies of the Magi had somehow got into her baggage.

*Ras* is a Norwegian word that denotes any mass of earth, snow, rock, ice, rubble or loose stone liable to fall on a traveller and crush his skull: notices with the phrase *Rasfare*, or danger from *ras*, are common in Oslo at the time of thaw when blocks of frozen snow fall from the steep roofs onto the pavements. Where roads are cut into the mountain, cars in all seasons, but especially in spring, are liable to be crushed by a falling mass before the driver is able to identify the particular form of landslide. Even the road to Hamar, the first town to the north of Oslo, was flagged with these signs.

There was snow still in May on the high ground above Oslo; the lakes were frozen, the air cold and the atmosphere, as it can only be in Norway, undefiled and fibrous after the winter frost. It was the first time I had driven a car in eight years, but after nine months in Oslo I was touched by the spring madness that afflicts all in Scandinavia. To attempt one of the worst road journeys in Europe after the severest Norwegian winter since 1812 was asking for misadventure. When I took leave of my escort, one of my first friends in Norway, who had piloted me to the city boundary, I was prepared to believe it was a final farewell.

Norwegian is usually considered a poor language, lacking the flexibility of Swedish or the richness of English. It uses an abundance of foreign words, yet when it comes to describing nature, there can be few languages that are more precise. Faith and belief are the same word in Norwegian, with a resulting confusion in theology. But there are at least ten words to denote a hill, according to its shape, size, steepness, the contours of its summit and the cultivation on it. The same holds of the moods of the sea, the texture of the snow, the layers of ice on the road.

Whenever I had spoken of my journey to friends they had smiled incredulously. It seemed to them a characteristic and crazy notion of a foreigner. No Norwegian would set out from Oslo in the spring to drive to Murmansk: he looks for adventure to the sea which has shaped his history and contributed most to his character. It has given him also a self-reliance which has affected even his religion.

In religious matters his Lutheran creed sits on him lightly. Ninety-six per cent of the people are officially members of the State Church, but that does not make them religious: church-going is confined to about three per cent over the entire country. Lutheranism in Norway has a comprehensiveness altogether different from Anglicanism. While no professed atheist would consider himself a member of the Church of England, he is absorbed without difficulty into the State Church system of Norway, along with every grade of unbeliever, disbeliever and misbeliever. The contradiction is not as great as it at first appears, for there is hardly a Norwegian who has not a residual appreciation of spiritual forces. Perhaps the inescapable grandeur of nature is responsible for it in the same way as the flat monotony of the Swedish countryside keeps its population largely earthbound.

An exhibit in the Kon-Tiki museum in Oslo gives a pointer to this. Exposed there is the journal of Thor Heyerdahl, the leader of the expedition. It is open at a passage, omitted in the printed book, which describes

*The Kon-Tiki raft*

the writer's fears when in a high sea he approached the coral reef lying out from the island on which he eventually landed. He writes in English:

> There were seconds I shall never forget. I thought of nothing but that all of us should hang on, hang on, hang, hang. And I asked a silent prayer. I know a couple of the other boys did the same. Others did not. To me it always gives an unidentifiable new supply of

strength and will. I am not a member of any Church by my own actions and I never visit them. But I know from this and many other experiences that there is something that can multiply my own limited powers [a] hundred times when I ask for it. Some people call it God. Others call it Tiki. I call it God. Be what it may, it helped me again to concentrate a stream of unidentifiable resources. And the roaring inferno thundered around!

There is one ubiquitous advantage of travel in Norway: every small town has a well-stocked book-shop and even hamlets provide a rack or two of paper-backs in the general store. Books are as essential to the Norwegian as Coca-Cola to the American. In the lower-class districts of English towns you can enter a row of houses without seeing more than the outdated encyclopedia which a clever pedlar has persuaded the occupant to buy on hire purchase, but in Norway, and particularly in the north, it is unusual to enter a poor home that has not several shelves of books: the more cultured and professional classes have their passages as well as their living-rooms lined with books from floor to ceiling. The very long winter nights explain the national habit of reading.

About half-way between Oslo and Hamar, before the bridge over the river Vorma, is a large white-timbered manor house, the home of Karsten Anker and one of the most historic buildings in Norway. It lies to the right of the road near the town of Eidsvoll which is hidden behind it. In this house the Norwegian Constitution was proclaimed on 17 May (now National Day) 1814.

In the previous January Denmark had been compelled to cede Norway to Sweden. Norway reacted by declaring her independence. Elections to a Constituent Assembly took place in church after Sunday services at which the congregation swore 'to defend Norway's independence and to sacrifice life and blood for their beloved country'. The hundred and twelve elected members to the Assembly met here in April and on 17 May announced their Constitution—an independent and limited monarchy under Prince Frederik of Denmark. Karsten Anker went over to London to elicit British support. He failed. A fortnight's war followed: the Swedes were repelled in the east, but succeeded in their march on Oslo from the south. Norway and Sweden became one kingdom, but the Constitution was saved; it was another ninety years before Norway became a separate kingdom under another Danish Prince, Håkon VII.

Karsten Anker's house is now a national monument. The decoration and furniture have been exactly restored. On the benches in the long hall are inscribed

*Eidsvoll manor house*

the names of the delegates and in a case is a duplicate handwritten copy of the Constitution. Its first Article is negative, excluding Jews, Gipsies, and Jesuits from residence in Norway.

# Hamar

Mjøsa, the largest inland lake in Norway, was still frozen on 10 May, as it had been for five months now. Everywhere Norwegians had complaints about the weather; it is a mistake to think that because their winter is hard, they like the cold or get used to it.

The churches off the roadside are enchantingly sited, often on an eminence encircled by silver birch, and illuminated at night. From a distance it is difficult to judge their age. Small Norwegian villages of the thirteenth century are still small today and their old stone churches have seldom been extended. The original proportions are unspoilt and have inspired the modern white-painted wooden churches of the country-side. Hideous ecclesiastical architecture is confined to the large towns: all but a few have vulgar or glaring red brick Gothic temples that never harmonise with their simple surroundings.

However, even in the cities graveyards are attractive. There is seldom more than a headstone, giving the date of birth and death. Occasionally a single phrase is added, *Takk for alt*, more rarely the old Catholic prayer for the dead, *Hvil i fred*, Rest in peace. On Christmas Eve, small sheltered lights, walled in by mounds of snow, are lit at each grave, as in Umbria on All Souls' Day. It is a custom that was killed in England at the Reformation but survived in Sweden and from there spread to Norway.

At Ottestad near Stange, less than nine kilometres before Hamar, stands an old country house now converted into a school, one of the two private boarding-schools in Norway. Only a rich endowment and high fees make it possible to meet State competition: it is evidence, seldom on the surface of Norwegian life, of the survival of a rich class in spite of the levelling process of taxation. The flat fee with extras equals a third of a professional man's untaxed income. The parents of the pupils are mostly on foreign service or posted abroad on business, though there are a few who simply believe in the benefits of private education.

Eckboskolen, called after its founder, was worth a visit. The main building is typical of the old country houses that few visitors to Norway ever see; the additions, which include the headmaster's suite, are in matching timber, but the *gård* or farm itself remains a fine example of the domestic architecture of the old upper classes: the frescoed walls, the decorative friezes, the painted ceilings and furniture, the well-proportioned rooms looking out on to Mjøsa make it possible to reconstruct a pre-Socialist way of life. The school domain has facilities for all the sports, including a ski-jump, skating-rink and shooting-range. The boys sleep in three-bunked rooms, their main meal is at three o'clock and a sauna bath is compulsory twice a week.

These large houses have barns on a matching scale. The Eckboskolen barn measures more than two hundred feet in length. Their plan is always the same, dictated by the need of getting all the animals, gear and fodder under shelter during winter. The ground floor houses cows, goats, pigs and sheep with farm machinery: in mid-May sixty cows and their calves were still there, waiting for the grass, brown after the snows, to turn green again. Housing animals is so expensive in Norway that until a few years ago there were only five thousand pigs in the country.

The barns are always built with an outside ramp leading to the top floor. Loaded carts drive up and tip their contents into compartments on both sides of the broad deck. Formerly dances and wedding feasts took place here; they would last for several days, and there was space enough on the long platform for scores of couples to eat, dance and sleep. In less grand houses the farm settlement is made up of several detached buildings—the living-house, stables, cook-house, barn, store-rooms, and sometimes even a schoolroom for the neighbourhood; in the nineteenth century, when old people were portioned out among the community, it often had its old resident pauper as well.

# Hamar

Hamar, an important town by Norwegian reckoning, is strategically placed at the approaches to Gudbrandsdalen, the main valley leading to middle and northern Norway; it protects also the west–east road linking the entries to the two narrower and parallel valleys of Østerdal and Trysil. The city itself dates from the time of St Olav. It has a tradition of independence notable even in Norway. In Viking days the kings would make occasional marches down Gudbrandsdalen and burn a *gård* or two, in order to keep the inhabitants in submission.

Hamar churchmen showed the same independence as the farmers: the resistance to the Lutheran Reformation was stubborn here. Old Bishop Mogens, its last Catholic bishop, armed himself to resist the German Lutheran invasion: he raised two copper cannons, two serpentines, a few muskets and some barrels of powder. But in the end he was taken captive to Denmark and died there in prison five years later. But it was only in his diocese that any Norwegian gave his life for the preservation of the old faith. Unfortunately little is known of them beyond the fact that they were leading citizens, owners of *gårds*. Everywhere in Norway the records of the Reformation are fragmentary; it is a great uncharted area of history.

In more recent times there was a stir in Hamar that rocked the State Church to its foundations.

On 25 January 1953 Professor Ole Hallesby, a leading Lutheran theologian, preached a broadcast sermon on the subject of eternal damnation. Addressing himself to listeners who were not 'reconciled' (in the Lutheran sense) to God, the Professor said: 'How can you, who are not repentant, dare to go to bed at night, not knowing whether you will wake up in bed or in Hell?'

The then Bishop of Hamar, Kristian Schjelderup, was not himself listening to the radio, but on learning what had been said, expressed his emphatic disagreement in a letter to *Aftenposten*: in his view Jesus was

merely echoing old Persian ideas of perpetual punishment for the wicked.

After the first exchange of letters in *Aftenposten*, the
controversy on the existence of Hell was taken up in
every journal and newspaper throughout Norway. No
subject had been discussed so vehemently since the trial
of Quisling. What emerged was the need of an authority
to speak in the name of the established Church.
Schjelderup himself challenged the Church to make
her position clear. In a letter to the Department for
Ecclesiastical Affairs, he asked whether his opinions
entitled him still to continue as Bishop of Hamar.

The Department is a government office, not a
doctrinal tribunal like the former Holy Office in Rome;
its head at the time was a social democrat, a fair-minded
atheist, who acted with exemplary rectitude. He referred
the challenge to the two Norwegian faculties of theology
and to the assembly of the eight Norwegian Bishops.
Their discussions continued to the end of the scholastic
year, when a cartoon appeared in an Oslo paper
depicting a traditional hell of fire, pitchforks and devils
with a notice, 'Closed for the vacation' above it. Later
the University theologians formulated an ambiguous
answer which enabled the Department to pronounce
that the issue of eternal punishment was not clear:
both opinions could co-exist in the Church and no
bishop or pastor could be deposed for teaching that
Hell did not exist. Schjelderup remained in office.

The discussion continued long after the decision had
been given. In the autumn of 1957, nearly five years
after the original broadcast, the Lutheran Church
assembly, without mentioning Schjelderup by name,
dissociated itself from his teaching. But before the
debate was forgotten, the authority of the Church
Assembly was itself questioned.

Schjelderup is now retired. In the immediate post-
war years he was a brave and forthright preacher,
prepared for unpopularity in his insistence on Christian

principles, a man, it would seem, sharing certain characteristics of a great Englishman, Nicholas Breakspeare, who founded his see of Hamar and later as Adrian IV became the only English Pope. A contemporary description of Breakspeare might well apply to Schjelderup: he was 'an extremely kindly man, gentle and restrained, ready of speech and an excellent preacher, slow to anger and a ready benefactor'.

Breakspeare, a contemporary of St Bernard and Abelard, was at the same school at Merton that St Thomas of Canterbury later attended. In 1152, five years after the foundation of Lysekloster and Hovedøya, he was sent to Norway as Papal Legate; he made the young Norwegian Church independent of the metropolitan jurisdiction of the Archbishop of Lund, then part of the Danish kingdom. Lund was replaced by Trondheim and Hamar, Schjelderup's see, added to the existing bishoprics of Oslo, Bergen and Stavanger.

With Breakspeare's brief visit begins the greatest period in the history both of the Church and of the country. From Norway he brought to the Papal throne in 1153 a predilection for conveying salutary teaching by means of a fable with a moral. All we know of him indicates that his teaching was as up-to-date as Schjelderup's eight centuries later. What he wrote of his own intellectual isolation and suffering might have been said by his successor today: he could imagine no man 'more pitiable or in worse estate'; the mental distress he experienced in office made him reckon all his previous unhappiness gaiety, all his earlier life as 'sheer felicity'. The Lord, he said, in a phrase that passed into an English proverb, had set him 'between the hammer and the anvil': Peter's chair was 'full of thorns, his mantle seeded with the sharpest needles'.

The large ruins of the Gothic cathedral at Hamar, on a nose of land protruding into Mjøsa about a mile north of the present town, is the principal reminder of

# Norway

Breakspeare's ecclesiastical rule in Norway: the fine line of stone piers, wholly Norman in structure, was unquestionably the work of the English craftsmen he introduced into Norway from his native country.

*Ruins of Hamar cathedral*

The modern cathedral above the lake in the centre of the town is interesting for the paintings behind the altar, the work of Sørensen, a gifted artist, less neurotic than Munch, to whom he holds second place in national esteem. The spirit of Breakspeare must be operative still in Hamar, for while the congregation that professes allegiance to the Papal See is diminutive, Schjelderup's successor, Bishop Johnson, is unique among Protestant prelates of any country in having two Catholic sisters (one of them a contemplative nun) as well as a brother and son in the Lutheran ministry.

There is nothing of secular interest in the town except the *White Swan of Mjøsa*, the oldest paddle-steamer in operation in Europe. Twice it has sunk to the bottom and been raised again, yet it turns out sprucely every spring to serve tourists who have the leisure to continue by water to Lillehammer at the north end of this inland sea.

# Hamar

Already barely a hundred miles north of Oslo this was a different world. There was something undefined and intangible, a hang-over from an unrecorded history, that made the visitor feel that Hamar was part of another Norway. Here as further south the constant refrain in conversation was still, 'the north is different'.

# CHAPTER 5

# LILLEHAMMER-GUDBRANDSDALEN-LOM-ÅNDALSNES

*O Springtime, springtime, save us!*
*No one has ever loved thee more tenderly than I . . .*
*Bear witness, ancient tree that I have worshipped thee*
*    even as a god,*
*Whose buds I have counted each spring more anxiously*
*    than pearls.*

Henrik Wergeland, 'To Spring'

Lillehammer is everyman's conception of what a Norwegian country town is like: trim, clean, prosperous, with lake, mountains and pastures, a tourist centre *par excellence* in winter and summer. There has been no vulgarisation and it preserves its own way of life independent of the tourist traffic.

The road there from Hamar is the continuation of the main artery between Oslo and the north; it runs a short way above Mjøsa through a pleasant wooded countryside.

In the middle of May the town was sleeping between seasons. The hotels were closed, the gift shops empty, the cafés taken over again by the natives. A spring mist sat on the lake; dark patches appeared on the surface of the cracking ice over which lorries had been driven during the hard winter.

Lillehammer has its own open-air museum similar to that at Bygdøy. It should be visited by all enthusiasts for Sigrid Undset, the novelist who adopted Lillehammer as her town. By arrangement with the Catholic priest or the tourist office in the town it is possible also to visit Undset's home, now occupied by her son and daughter-in-law.

Undset's father, Ingval Undset, was from Trondheim, her mother from Denmark where she was born in 1882. To the historian and sociologist her novels give a remarkable penetration into the Norwegian character. Better than anyone in her day she understood the pessimism that began to depress Norwegians at the very time, ironically, they won their independence from Sweden in 1905. Her first novel, *Fru Martha Oulie*, set in the Oslo of that day, was published two years later. She portrays the ordinary middle-class people—a well-defined section before the onset of Socialism—earning their living in offices, vacillating already in the fortunes of their marriages. The sinews of the old Norwegian society were beginning to crack. Relative morality was replacing an unquestioned code of behaviour inextricably tied to a religion that was now losing its hold on the people.

Sigrid Undset was the first Norwegian writer of stature to observe the selfish individualism that this changed society produced. The gloomy story of Jenny, in her novel of that name, gives a picture valid today of the lonely, isolated Norwegian, ill-equipped for life, vainly searching for something she knows not what.

This insight, almost uncanny in its definition, is the strength of her early writings. Like numberless Norwegians today, she was an atheist at the start, but unlike them realised the silliness of a label that was attached mainly to deists who had a private quarrel with God. Again she was typical of them in rejecting Christianity without becoming positively anti-Christian. To her young generation the State Church seemed even then unrealistic in its approach to the human problem.

It is a measure of Undset's greatness that her historical novels are paradoxically modern in all but their setting. Unlike Walter Scott she is not subject to literary fashion. It surprised Norwegians that her

second book, *Viga-Ljot og Vigdis*, placed at the end of
the tenth century, was as realistic as her first. She had
already mastered the most difficult form of fiction.

Her father was a leading Norwegian archaeologist.
When only ten years old she used to read to him old
Norsk sagas and legends during his last sickness. It
was not that she switched from ancient to modern and
back again: she was truthful to a Norwegian mood,
constant in its ingredients and altering only in its
reaction to the centuries. In the end she could foresee
little but suicide for the society she loved; developments
since her death have not greatly altered her prognosis.

In 1924, in mid-course of her literary career, she
became a Catholic. The Lutheran Church never had a
strong appeal to her for the reasons that it has lost its
appeal to most Norwegians today: it is a State Church.
St Thomas More was her hero more than St Olav: a
man who had foreseen more clearly than any person in
history the results of this subordination. Critics agree
that her greatest series of novels, *Kristin Lavransdatter*,
followed her acceptance of the religion that concided
with the finest centuries in Norwegian history. In her
appreciation of Catholicism she showed a perspicacity
rare among her fellow-countrymen.

In 1919 she moved from Oslo to Lillehammer. Her
house is on the fringe of the town, an old peasant's
home dating from about 1720, transferred from Dalseg
in Gudbrandsdalen. It is similar to the houses to be seen
in the Lillehammer open-air museum, except that it is
lived in. The *stuer* or living-rooms, and study are as they
were in her time and her library has been kept intact:
shelves of Belloc, Knox, Baring and Chesterton, the
English mystics and martyrs, Gasquet, More, all the
works that marked the Catholic revival in England during the 'thirties; and alongside them the main source
book of the Norwegian lore, the volumes of *Norges Land
og Folk*. In the garden were the *akagebaer* she herself
had planted.

# Gudbrandsdalen

A few kilometres beyond Lillehammer at the north end of Mjøsa the road enters Gudbrandsdalen. On this overcast May afternoon the opening to the pass appeared grey and grave, even menacing. Clouds clung low on the mountainsides; the road was rough and broken after the winter frost. This was the gorge of the River Lågen and it lured the traveller into what seemed the heart of Norway, though in fact it was still the south. A friend in Lillehammer had reminded me as I left him: 'It is full winter on the mountain range south of Bodø.'

There are certain passes in the world that hold the key to the history of whole countries: Roncesvalles in the Pyrenees, the Khyber Pass, the Brenner and, here in Norway, Gudbrandsdalen. It is the inescapable line of conquest or retreat and the power that holds it is dominant. From the time of St Olav in the eleventh century to the German campaign in the spring of 1940, Gudbrandsdalen has been the main artery of the kingdom. There are valleys that join it from the west, but to the east there is only a mountain barrier. A tourist, sensitive to the mood of a place, even if he has no knowledge of the history of Norway, feels at once that it must all lie here in this dark gorge. Every broader space into which the valley opens at intervals has its list of military engagements: a rearguard action by the ill-equipped British forces or a punitive raid by a Norwegian king.

In the churches in the southern part of Gudbrandsdalen it is possible to trace the progress of the Danish King, Kristian IV, the brother of Anne, James I's consort, from Oslo to Trondheim in 1639. He made his way up the valley in wagons. In every hamlet he was greeted by local bards and passed under a triumphal arch. The burden of entertainment fell on the small communities who remembered the simple-minded monarch as the man who took their goods without paying for them. It was the same king who considered it his special mission, entrusted to him by his father, Frederick

II, to campaign in Norway and Denmark against all forms of amusement. Dancing, smoking, operas were condemned, laughing was considered sinful, comedians, jugglers, finambulists were exiled. Norwegian peasants who failed to attend Sunday church were placed in the stocks.

Pietism was not the King's creation. It originated in the valleys north and west of Bergen in an endeavour to improve morals. It clouded religion with an impenetrable gloom, arrested the growth of dramatic art, almost killed the first stirrings of a literary revival in Norway. Holberg, the first great figure in modern Norwegian literature, a native of Bergen, who lived most of his life in Copenhagen, wrote twenty-eight plays in the six years before the Danish theatre was closed in 1728, and none in the next twenty.

At Fåvang the Lutheran Minister congratulated me on my Norwegian and told me I was the first tourist of the year. His stave church had a fine carved crucifix

*Urnes stave church*

which he ascribed to the seventeenth century but agreed with me that it might well belong to Catholic times. Here also and a little further up the valley in the stave church at Ringebu, the royal Danish arms commemorated King Kristian's progress. In both places the chalice lay on the altar, as is usual in Lutheran churches. Metaphysical distinctions between Catholic and Lutheran belief in the Eucharist are illustrated by the treatment of the sacrament: the dregs of the wine or (in some places) fruit juice are left in the small cups in the sacristy until the sexton washes up later in the week; then too any altarbreads left over from the Sunday celebration are replaced in the sacristy cupboard. To the Catholic who believes in an enduring Eucharistic Presence these customs underline a totally different approach to the central sacrament of the Christian life.

Yet it is the Lutheran not the Catholic churches in Norway that are invariably locked: the key can usually be had at the nearest house or farm. At Ringebu a grave-digger told me he had left the side door open and I could slip in through it. Inside were an interesting picture of St Laurence and some fine painted woodwork. The early nineteenth-century restoration had been confined mainly to the outside structure.

There were farms set high on the mountains in forest clearings all the way up this valley. The sun reaches them many weeks earlier than the farms below. They are occupied all the year round, and higher still, but used only in summer, were the Norwegian *seters* or summer farms. In any drive across the mountains these *seters* can be seen, either singly or in a group of three or four, set usually in the hollow of the plateau. They are attached always to a *gård* in the valley. At the end of winter cows and goats are driven there and stay for three or four months. The *seter* building is usually a one-storied hut with two rooms: the family lives in the anteroom; beyond is the dairy, where cheeses are manufactured. Sometimes a *seter* may be twenty or more miles from the *gård* to which it belongs.

Otta, a hundred and seventy-eight kilometres north of Hamar, is an important junction of valleys. Less than a mile before the town a curious memorial, a few feet above the road to the right, unexpectedly links Gudbrandsdalen with Scotland. It marks the place where a troop of Scottish mercenaries under Captain Sinclair was destroyed by the Norwegian peasantry in 1612. The force, possibly 500 men, raised in Scotland for service in Sweden, had anchored on 20 August in the west, in Romsdalsfjord, near a cliff called Skothammaren, then crossed the mountains into Gudbrandsdalen. Here at Kringen the local peasants, who were prepared for its approach, took up their position on the hillside above the road that runs parallel with the river Lågen. The memorial in stone shows their leader, a girl, Pillar Guri, giving a blast on her horn. This was the signal for the natives in ambush in the hills above the pass to hurl down upon the Scots boulders and felled trees. Many Scots who were not killed outright were drowned in the river. The advance guard, which had been allowed to pass, surrendered and was slaughtered. Sinclair fell. Only eighteen men, mostly officers, were taken to Akershus, then to Copenhagen. The episode is significant because it kindled national patriotism. A translation of some lines of one of many poems written to celebrate the event reads:

> *Among the rocks in the north, on this very spot,*
> *A fully armed corps of some hundred Scots*
> *Was here crushed to death like earthen pots.*

It would seem that the dead were stripped of their clothing, for in this part of the valley today the national dress nearly resembles a Scottish tartan: it is not the Sinclair tartan but is close to the McAlister. At the time of the disaster clan tartans had barely, if at all, developed, although regional tartans were in existence.

Ottadal, the valley to the east, leads through Lom and through a pass onto Sognefjell and then south via Hardanger and Voss to Bergen. Here is the heart of

# Lom

Norway. At Vågå, the first town west of Otta on the road to Lom, there is an historic *gård*, Sandbu. Locally it is

*Sandbu Gård near Vågå*

thought that it was at one time a monastery, at another a royal residence. Certainly it is established that the twelfth-century owners, the Gjesling family, were close friends of King Sverre Sigurdsson, but the exact history of the place has been irretrievably lost. Today members of the Gjesling family live still on part of the property which was divided about the year 1400.

A triangle taken with Vågå at its apex and a line between Bergen and Molde at its base encloses some of the finest scenery south of Trondheim—fjords, glaciers, salmon rivers and mountain plateaus, and also the stave churches of Lom itself, Urnes, Vik and other hamlets. From the summit of Sognefjell there is a view of the highest mountain range of Norway, with the peak of the Glittertind in the near distance. In May this road is closed; it is at its best in the brief autumn fortnight in mid-October: the roads are still passable, the tourists are gone, there is sun, elk meat and forests of birch and mountain ash in every depth of bronze and gold. It is good to be at large and at leisure in this vast area before the snows bar it in. Every valley off the main route is worth entering; each has its individual unrepeated charm. Bøverdalen at the start of the ascent of Sognefjell is well known, and there is a road, high above the tree line, that leaves the Lom road twenty kilometres before the town, passing over the mountain plateau to the east of Glittertind and south through the Valdres valley back to Oslo. But, as in other districts of the south, when it comes to scenic glory each man has endless opportunity to follow his preference or mood. There is always some valley that responds to them.

The area round Lom is one of the most remote fastnesses of Norway where the Catholic religion died slowly. There are virtually no written records of the usurpation; in small hamlets, isolated farms and old homes it is possible to pick up shreds of legends that can never be confirmed. In the narrow ravine that leads from Lom to Sognefjell, on the far side of the mountain stream, there is a strikingly regular cavity in the rocks, divided into two chambers. It is known locally as the Troll church. It is said to have been a secret meeting place for Mass when the new Lutheran minister, German trained, took over Lom church from the last Catholic priest. But the tradition cannot be substantiated. Undoubtedly the old religion lingered: the last remnants of it were certain practices that had long ceased to have any acknowledged association with it. Even at the end of the nineteenth century there were peasants who still prayed on their beads; others who, asked who was the head of the Church, would answer the Pope. The present-day custom of eating cod on Christmas eve, found in Bergen and the west, is thought to be a survival of the Catholic abstinence from meat on this vigil. In other places in the west parents taking their children to be christened dipped their finger in the salt fjord water and then passed it over the

lips of the infant: this was in lieu of the salt adminis-
tered in the old Catholic rite of baptism which was done
away with at the Reformation.

But equally hazy are the surviving prejudices. No one
has yet been able to explain satisfactorily the origin of
the belief that lingers still even among educated Norwegians that a Protestant entering a Catholic church
will be swept out with a broom before Mass begins
by a nun singing as she sweeps, 'Thus we sweep the
sinners out!' The fable is thought to derive from the
rite of blessing with the *Asperges* that customarily
preceded the principal Mass. In remote places Catholics
are still regarded as a species of unbelievers. That they
have a sacrament of confirmation is a revelation to most
Norwegians.

Here at Otta, where Gudbrandsdalen broadened into
a plain, the sun was already up at 6.15 in the middle of
May. As in all hotels, breakfast was laid out like a
buffet banquet: trout, salmon, sardines, cold meats—
reindeer, beef, pork—cheese board, fruit, fresh, stewed
and canned. After such a start it is no hardship to drive
the rest of the day with only a sandwich at noon.
Breakfast in the hotel at Otta was a reminder that,
though Norway may be connected geographically with
the mainland of Europe, it is not the Continent. That
begins at Copenhagen.

The river was gurgling with noisy thick yellow mud.
At eight o'clock the road continuing up Gudbrandsdalen
was clear of traffic, the camping sites were closed for
the winter, there was no sign of church-going in the
valley. At Dovre, the name also of the mountain beyond
Dombås on the road to Trondheim, there was a
church, constructed entirely of slates, that was unique
in Norway, if not in Europe. A thick rainbow came
down to the floor of Gudbrandsdalen which was grander
here than to the south.

At Dombås, 47 kilometres north of Otta, there was a
choice of routes. The river Lågen turns here to the west,

then passes over the hills to Romsdal and to the coast at Åndalsnes, while the main road continues north over Dovrefjell and on to Trondheim. On the far side of the fjell it is possible to turn east and reach Trondheim via Røros, one of the most attractive old towns in Norway. Behind the choice of routes was the further question: where to spend the Seventeenth May, the Norwegian national day commemorating the signing of the first Constitution in 1814 at Eidsvoll.

At Dombås I was still undecided. I had an introduction to one of the best-known citizens of Åndalsnes: one introduction might lead to another and I would be certain of company on the Seventeenth May. My old Baedeker was lyrical about the road to Åndalsnes; I had crossed Dovrefjell two years earlier; Røros could be taken in on my return journey. Therefore I swung to the west. After a few miles I had no regrets.

Nobody knows Gudsbrandsdalen who has not followed it beyond Dombås. In Oslo I had been prepared for its beauty: it had even been suggested that I should garage my car in Dombås and continue to Åndalsnes by train so as to take in the beauty of the valley without distraction. From the road that was cut high up on the northern slope of the Lågen valley, the countryside was laid out like an idealistic scene set for a Flemish madonna: it had the same detail, precision, fusion of colour, with river, low-lying pasture, historic barns surmounted by belfries, white-timbered churches, turf-roofed houses, pine forests, blue hills and in the distance snow-covered mountains. At this time of the year it was possible to drive slowly and take in a scene that was sufficient for a single memorable visit to Norway. The pleasure alters in shade as each curve of the road gives a fresh viewpoint.

Memorials commonly multiply in countries that are young or, as with Norway, have an ancient history of independence, interrupted for centuries and resumed only in recent times. A friend, at the time Editor of *The*

# Åndalsnes

*Times Literary Supplement*, after a lecture in Oslo was asked the age of the paper he represented. His answer 'as old as your country' was not the most tactful, for Norwegians can claim to have conquered Dublin before England was a single kingdom and discovered North America seven centuries before Columbus. Here in the upper Lågen valley, at Lesjaskog, were two stone slabs planted proudly in the ground to commemorate two incidents in the Norwegian saga against oppressor nations: the first to the Norwegians killed in the Napoleonic wars (1807–1814), the second to the dead of the second World War.

Åndalsnes was the base of General Paget's expeditionary force in April 1940. For lack of an airfield he used the frozen lake below this memorial. Among the names on the slab were C. W. Jenning, P. Rankin, G. Twiby and Wolsow: men of the R.A.F. ground staff who had attempted for an heroic forty-eight hours to keep planes in service while the ice-field was being pitted by German bombs.

Few buildings in the Norwegian countryside are old, but in this valley there were farms that were on the site of *gårds* mentioned in the earliest sagas. The lie of the land, the angle of the first sun to reach the valley, the shelter given by the mountains, are the unchanging factors that give these places authenticity. Much Norwegian history, legend and fable can be discovered under the steeply-sloping roof of comparatively recent buildings, sometimes also relics of a more recent past, tapestries, silver, an occasional painting, domestic furnishing dating from the seventeenth century or earlier. The Norwegians are basically peasants, in no pejorative sense, and their culture is a peasant culture; their crafts too, particularly their woodcarving and painting, are peasant crafts. The country mansions, though some exist and today are turned to State uses, are rare. At Einbu, some four kilometres beyond the memorials at Lesjaskog, there is St Olav's farm. This was the valley in which he, like General Paget, had campaigned.

*Detail of calvary group in Urnes church*

The road, passing into Romsdal, follows a ravine falling steeply to sea-level at Åndalsnes. Here there was a sudden burst of spring: young fresh leaves, grass that was green not brown, flowers among the snow that still lay in cavities of the rock even at low levels. Over the lip of the mountains, on either side, for a stretch of several miles, there were waterfalls, single cascades, splintering jets, broad single sheets of water, all noisy and heavy from the prodigious mass of melting winter ice. Where there was any arable land, stone walls, seen only here and in the province of Rogaland in which Stavanger lies, divided it neatly as in the Lake District of England. It was possible to feel almost instantly the mildness that the Gulf Stream brings to the west coast of Norway.

It was the eve of the Seventeenth May. There is no day like it in the world. It is the national holiday above all others, in which all join. It commemorates not the comparatively recent separation from Sweden, but the 1814 Constitution drawn up at Eidsvold, which Sweden later recognised and which gave Norway limited independence under the Swedish crown.

# Åndalsnes

At Åndalsnes the next morning bangers were let off in the street at 4.30. The sun was up and almost warm. Half an hour later rattles, cheering, songs, transistor radios, automobile horns, trumpets, whistles had created a din in which no deaf man could remain asleep. A truck trailing a string of empty cans, with a boy's brass band on board, drove fiendishly up and down the outlying streets; ships on the quay blew their sirens; everything that could contribute to the noise was used. There was no doubt that the Seventeenth May had dawned.

In the two hours' wait for breakfast in the hotel I watched processions of children, each led by a band, march eight abreast down to the station square: girls in white frocks edged with emerald, and with matching emerald bonnets, waving canes decorated with emerald ribbons, the boys with emerald ties and berets, or in black trousers with emerald stripes. This was the youth of Åndalsnes that had graduated from the *Realskole* to the Gymnasium. The younger children were un-uniformed but all tirelessly waved small Norwegian flags. From this day until the close of term a month later they kept their emerald gear. In larger towns older girls and boys, who had graduated from the Gymnasium—there was no Gymnasium here—wore red caps, ties, scarves or trousers. These are the *Russ*. A month of dancing and social engagements, and often a visit to Denmark, follows their emancipation.

The early morning noises were the first item on the programme: they were described as 'Salute: Music in the Streets'. The *barnetoget*—literally, children's procession—formed up about 9 a.m. from these converging groups for a united march to the small octagonal church of Veblungsnes about two miles across the sound. It was led by the local Seventeenth of May committee (on to which I had been co-opted in the course of breakfast at the hotel) and was brought up in the rear by the flag-bearer, pursued by a rabble of children not yet of school age. Parents and the general populace straggled behind. A few were in the national dress of the district—in tight-waisted jackets, with bright buttons, breeches and silver shirt studs.

Allegedly there was a children's service here but it was only the infants with no option who attended it. The rest broke up into untidy groups, sucked *dola-ice*, sat on the churchyard fence, listened on transistors to the celebrations in Trondheim, Oslo and Røros: there were sermons from the Cathedral churches, recorded extracts from Churchill's speech on his first post-war visit to Oslo, national songs, more brass bands.

It resembled more a festival of spring than a commemoration of national independence. The exuberance was heightened by the anticipation of summer. In the less formal afternoon march the schoolchildren used floats and banners to register their comments on drink, sex and the government: 'Let them have topless, we will have bottomless', and others of more local pertinence. The tail of this second march was brought up by a medley of townspeople, by all who wanted to march, as the programme stated, and had not yet done so. It was curious to see small boys wearing sometimes three rows of ribbons.

There was a formal address the same afternoon in the grounds of the Grand Hotel. The speaker was a dull local worthy who wore a black hangman's cap with string and tassels coming down over his shoulders. It was like the opening of an English garden party in aid of a new church organ. A gymnastic display followed, then songs and recitals, and finally a dance in the school hall at which all the girls wore short frocks.

After the Seventeenth May the new year begins in Norway.

# CHAPTER 6
# ROMSDAL-MOLDE

*The modern Norwegian has assimilated Christianity,
but has not altogether outlived the Viking strain.*

Konsul Jonas Lied, *Return to Happiness* (1943)

Troll is a generic word used for every species of wizard resident and operative in country places in Norway. Even on the briefest visit a tourist comes across a dozen place-names that begin with 'troll': in the index of the gazetteer there are several columns of such names. To take only the most obvious: Troll-vik (hamlet), Trolløya (island), Troll-stua (-room), Troll-dalen (-valley), Troll-fjellet (mountain), Troll-elva (-river), Trollfjord. But in addition to the official list, there are all the Troll-sites, like Trollkirke (-church) in the previous chapter, that exist only in local tradition.

Here in the neighbourhood of Åndalsnes is Trolltin-dane, a weird, almost grotesque, range of peaks that looks like an array of trolls squatting menacingly over the valley. Its scarred and stained grey walls rise sheer from the floor to the sky as steeply as any mountains in the world. The legend is that a number of trolls established their home on this range and waged an intermittent war with the gnomes in the valley below. They adopted the same strategy as the Norwegian peasants who crushed Sinclair's men at Kringen: they lay hidden until the gnomes appeared at the base of the mountain, when they rolled down masses of rock and stone. But the trolls, who were permitted to operate only at night, were lured out at midday and for their indiscretion were turned into these jagged peaks.

Any peasant in Norway can tell the visitor the troll legends associated with the natural features of his valley. I have sat and listened to these tales in friends'

houses in southern Norway. Some have been assembled
in books, others still live on unwritten. This lore and
legend is something peculiarly Norwegian. The trolls of
Sweden and Denmark belong to a different race.
Like the modern Norwegian the troll conforms to no
established pattern of behaviour. He acts at times with
justice; always he is awesome. His stupidity leads in the
end to his defeat, either by man or gnomes or by
Askeladden, the hero of the folk-tales.

After Norwegian jerseys the most popular souvenirs
of a visit to Norway are the carved and painted wooden
trolls. There are well-known shops in Karl Johansgate
that stock both; but when it comes to buying trolls the
tourist needs instruction. After the ordinary troll,
*trollus ordinarius* as he can be called, comes the *draug*,
represented usually as a bundle of sea wrack, for this is
how he has been observed close at hand by mariners.
He is the sea troll, invariably sinister: his appearance is
an omen of impending shipwreck. A near cousin of the
same name operates ordinarily on the coast: if inadvertently he is taken on board, he overturns the
boat.

But the troll family embraces also *huldrefolk*, the
*nisse, hauge, sluagh, merman, mermaid*, the *nøkk, fosse-
grime, jutuls* and others. The *oskurei* are a whole pack
of such creatures that ride noisily in the air; popularly
they are called *åsgårdsreier*. In everyday life it is
necessary to be familiar only with the *nisse*, who if given
the attention he demands is normally friendly. At
Christmas on the country farms he expects a bowl of
porridge and will cause irritation if he does not get it.
In the shape of the *Julenisse* (or Christmas *nisse*) he is the
ancestor of the Anglo-Saxon Father Christmas, along
with St Nicholas.

The folk-tales and the unwritten legends, in which the
troll figures, present the Norwegians as an independent,
self-reliant people, such as might be expected in a
country where the livelihood of the peasants was at the

mercy of nature. Their humour is often earthy. Churchmen, the King, the local powers are treated with little respect.

The troll world existed before the days of St Olav; it is a world of witchcraft, curses and personalised forces of nature, over which presided Odin, the master of magic, who possessed spells suited to every contingency. It survived the coming of Catholicism in the tenth century and, mingling with it, continued into the Lutheran era. Unexplained phenomena are attributed to

*Nøkken*

the distant action of trolls, even when they make no personal appearance. The same blend of Christian and pagan beliefs is found also in ghost stories, for instance in the variants of the tale of the trolls' midnight Mass in Møllergaten in Oslo. An old lady, who intended to go to an early morning service on Christmas Day, woke at night to find her clock had stopped. The hands stood at 11.30, the moon was shining onto the floor of her bedroom and from her window she saw the church lit up. She took her prayer-book and went out.

71

# Norway

The streets were quiet; she sat in her usual pew, but when she looked round, she thought the people seemed pale and strange. There was no worshipper she knew, but there were many she thought she had met before. When the pastor went up to the pulpit, she did not recognise him as one of the city's ministers. He was a tall, pale man and she thought somehow she knew him too. He preached well, but there was not the noise, coughing and clearing of throats usual during the early service on Christmas morning. The silence made her uneasy.

As the congregation started to sing, a woman sitting beside her leaned over and whispered in her ear, 'Throw your coat loosely over your shoulders and go. If you stay here until the end, you will be ruined. It is the dead who are holding the service.'

She glanced at the woman and recognised her. It was her neighbour who had died many years ago. Then, as she cast her eyes about the church again, she remembered the faces of the congregation. They had all died long ago.

She turned to leave. They grabbed her. At the church steps they took hold of her coat. She let it go. The church clock struck one as she passed through the door into the street.

In the morning she came to the church again. Her coat was lying there, a short pink cloth coat with a rabbit lining.

A prison now stands in Møllergaten; no midnight service is held even today in the Lutheran church; the souls of the dead are associated with the folk of the troll legends.

As impressive as Trolltindane near Åndalsnes is the zigzag road, Trollstigveien, the troll steps, cut like a giant's footprints through a pass that goes south over the mountains to Norddalsfjord. In May it was closed but in mid-summer it is a nerve-testing tourist attraction. Also near Åndalsnes is Romsdalshorn, with its slippery wall terminating in a tower-shaped peak, still reckoned one of the four or five most difficult climbs in Europe. And there are valleys of indescribable beauty off the main roads in all this area.

Before a cross-country journey in spring it is well to enquire the state of the roads. Reliable information is hard to come by, partly because the estimation of a good road varies. After a severe winter there is always an element of adventure in taking a secondary road.

Communications or the lack of them are another difficulty. Norwegian country life is a life of valleys in which people live their own lives enclosed by mountain walls. In the Norwegian campaign of 1940 General Paget, the British commander, had his base at Åndalsnes. His information was bad and there was no means of checking it except by costly experience. The instructions given to him were to proceed up Romsdal into Gudbrandsdalen, then over Dovrefjell, and to hold Trondheim, thus cutting off the north from the south. His base at Åndalsnes was ill chosen for a modern military operation. Enemy aeroplanes appeared over it with only two minutes' warning from behind the peaks of Trolltindane, Romsdalshorn and other mountains that hugged the town. There was the inevitable evacuation conducted with brilliant seamanship. When the last warship steamed out of the fjord, an immense column of smoke curled miles up into the sky. The town is now totally rebuilt.

Distances on the map deceive most first-time tourists in Norway. Mileage reckoned at home for day-to-day driving should be cut by half. It is true that many of the roads are finely engineered, but great yearly damage is done to their surface by the winter frost. Repair squads are at work everywhere between May and September. Few roads follow the valley for long before zigzagging up a mountain pass; there are long delays for ferries and obstructions without number. Hardly any motorist who sets out from Oslo for

Hammerfest reaches his destination. An English friend of mine who had done the journey was not such a madman as his friends maintained when he turned in his new car for an old one before heading north.

In the comparatively short distance between Åndalsnes and Molde there were two ferries. Across the first at Sølsnes lived a local worthy, one of the last of the *små konger* or 'small kings', unrecognised as such by law but nevertheless, as his peers in Viking days, the sovereign of the district. I was fortunate in having an introduction to him. His old wooden *gård* stood on the hill above the landing stage, about five hundred yards down the road opposite the church.

Konsul Jonas Lied, then eighty-six, lived in isolated majesty. His name was mentioned with awe by the small boys from the neighbouring farm, by the garage attendant, by the men operating the ferry.

Lied was prepared for my visit. He was a man of instant authority. His welcome was cool but courteous; but as I came to admire him, his reserve was put aside. Bespectacled, withdrawn, light-skinned, studious-looking and wiry, he was in the tradition of men like Amundsen, Nansen and Thor Heyerdahl. His mother's family had lived here since 1350: he showed me the old loom by which they had spun their livelihood. In a specially fitted glass-paned cabinet were five shelves of the uniformly bound volumes of the diary which he had kept without the omission of a single day since he was a youth. The cabinet was already inscribed as his gift to the maritime museum in Bygdøy, Oslo, to which he had bequeathed it under the terms of his will.

Konsul Lied claimed that he lived in the most beautiful place in the world and, as he told me later, he had travelled three times round the world. From his garden he looked over the Veøy, perhaps the most historic island in Norway, comparable in its associations to Iona. Now virtually uninhabited, Veøy lay in the shape of an exclamation mark about a mile off-shore from the ferry terminus. Its only surviving church, where Konsul Lied had been christened, was, after Muster near Haugesund, the oldest in Norway. Built first in wood in 1050 on the site of a temple dedicated to Odin and Thor, it had been reconstructed in stone a hundred years later. The island was, so to speak, the heart of the saga country. In Viking days it had an important market which was the largest trading centre between Trondheim and Bergen. It was the first place in Norway to receive Christianity, introduced from Ireland after the Viking raids on Dublin: from here an Irish priest made his way north-east to Trondheim and became the first bishop in Norway. Konsul Lied showed me a photograph album of the island with his own typed history of the place on facing pages. It was a copy of the volume which he had sent to Queen Elizabeth II, whose family, he claimed, originated in Veøy. The letter of thanks from Buckingham Palace was dated November 1964.

William the Conqueror was sixth in line of descent from the Viking, Jarl Rangvald, the father of Rollo the Ganger, the ally of King Harald Fairhair, who after the battle of Hafrsfjorden, achieved the unity of Norway on Veøy and made the island a symbol of it. Rollo then sailed for Normandy about 874, and from there Duke William, his great-great-grandson, crossed to England two hundred years later.

Konsul Lied, unprofessional, industrious and self-taught, had made this tract of Norwegian-Norman history his special study. In his library were rare books on the subject, mostly in French, which he had bought in antiquarian bookshops in Rouen.

Konsul Lied's main claim to fame lay in his discovery of a trading passage through the polar seas to Siberia; he was backed by Commander Christensen from Sandefjord and financed by Alfred Derry of Derry & Toms, the Kensington store. In 1911 he established his headquarters at Krasnoiyarsk, a city of traders, trappers and exploiters on the Yenesi river which flows from the heart of Siberia to the Arctic. The next year, in the Grand Hotel in Oslo, the Siberian Steamship Manufacturing and Trading Company was founded. To give publicity to his venture he persuaded Nansen to sail with him in the *Correct* from Tromsø in order to load and carry to Atlantic ports the wares—mostly furs, soft leather and embroidery—he had accumulated at Novonosky. The *Correct* followed the course previously charted by the *Fram* along the Siberian coast. Lied nearly lost his life when an ice-floe on which he went hunting walruses was caught in a strong current. He was rescued by Nansen who became his life-long friend: a man, as he described him, who had a distant look as if he always saw ice-floes from his living-room. By the

*Fridtjof Nansen*

outbreak of the Russian Revolution his Company owned eighty river steamers and three hundred barges and was well set to outstrip in the ramifications of its trade the great Hudson's Bay Company. The Konsul maintained that in natural resources Siberia was the richest country in the world.

As he took me round his house he showed me a mammoth's tusk 50,000 years old discovered in the arctic ice: he had recovered the entire beast. Except in parts where dogs and wolves had made incisions it was well preserved and there was magnificent shaggy brown hair under its head. Eighty reindeer hauled it up the frozen Yenesi river to the nearest point of the trans-Siberian railway for the transportation to St Petersburg. Lied had kept this tusk and some teeth.

In the same room there were ikons from the fourteenth century, painted on curved wood to prevent destruction by microbes, and photographs, some of them taken by himself, of noted Russians, including Rasputin, in the last days of the Czars. Signed photographs of the Grand Duke Andrew and other Romanoffs were relics of his friendship with them. In August 1917 when the royal family was moved to Tobolsk in Siberia, Lied, who was operating in the district, visited England and, in conjunction with the Grand Duke Michael, made a plan to rescue them by his arctic sea route, but the Czar was removed before it could be put into effect. He showed me a porcelain dish with a portrait of the Russian royal family which he asserted was the last likeness made from life. The Konsul dismissed abruptly my query on the survival of the Princess Anastasia. 'The Bolsheviks always did a thorough job', he said decisively.

It was amazing what treasures he had been able to bring out of Russia at the time of the Revolution: all his Russian silver, some thirty-three original paintings of early St Petersburg and his diary. In Moscow he had discussed the business of his Company with both Lenin and Trotsky. Lenin, he judged, had no time for anyone of Lied's type.

Konsul Lied invited me to a meal, but I had to get on my way. Pastor Henriksen, the local Lutheran minister, came in. He had spent some hours, at Lied's request, trying to get a boat for me over to Veøy, but unavailingly. Both assured me that nothing of interest remained on the island except the old church: forest had usurped the rest of the island's past. The rain was heavy. I promised myself that on another visit I would leave more time to explore Langfjord, this protected and almost sacred inlet of Moldefjord. As I skimmed back over the pages of the visitors' book, which the Konsul gave me to sign, I noticed several distinguished names. I asked the old man about Field-Marshal Auchinleck: he had been the Konsul's guest after the war.

The mist was thick on the surface of the fjord. There could be no question of a photograph. Pastor Henriksen piloted me in his Volkswagen on to the road leading to the next ferry. When I took my leave of him, he told me that he was an admirer of my fellow-Jesuit, St Francis Xavier. I thought at first he had said he himself was called Francis Xavier: but this was an inconceivable name, as he explained, for a Norwegian. 'Is Konsul Lied a faithful member of your flock?' I asked him. 'No,' he answered, 'he has his own philosophy.'

Molde lies ten kilometres beyond the terminus of the next ferry. For a newly-rebuilt town it has a charm lacking in a score of other rebuilt coastal towns further north. It was from here that the Norwegian gold was dispatched to England in April 1940 as the Germans pushed north. Both the new Lutheran and the new Catholic church are in a good modern style, which is evident also in the shopping centre. A *foss* or waterfall running down the hill through the centre of the town is skirted with gardens. There are vistas from the high street out onto the dark skerries scattered in the fjord.

It is legend, fostered by travel agents, that the Norwegians are a handsome people, that the Swede is necessarily fair-skinned and blond, the Finn a near albino. As a people, the Norwegians are probably less good-looking than the English, though Norwegian women are often startlingly beautiful. Fine features endure many centuries and recur at intervals of several generations. In the tenth century the Vikings brought back with them from Ireland, France and England the best appointed girls as the prize of war; even after a reversal of arms they put them aboard, for they never moved far from the rivers which gave them a quick line of retreat to the sea where their enemies could not follow them.

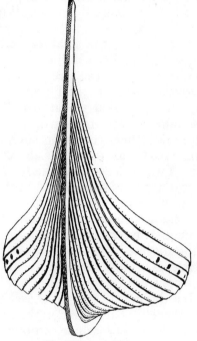

*The Gokstad Ship*

In Molde I was struck, as I had not been in any other place or district in Norway, by the fine features of the ordinary people in the streets and cafés: these inlets of the fjords, the heart of the old Viking country, must have seen ten centuries ago many fair damsels step ashore from the high-prowed ships.

After Molde my next stopping-place was Trondheim. I planned to hop the distance by sea, for it was still early in the year and I could get no certain information of the condition of the road through the valley of Sunndalen to Oppdal and the familiar northern road that I had left at Dombås. In any case it was my intention then to drive through this valley on my return, when the seasonal repairs to the road surface would make it less hazardous. The district to the west of Molde was known as Trollheimen, the home of the trolls.

I settled therefore for the steamer and had my first brief contact with the tourist industry.

The *Finnmark*, one of the fleet of coastal steamers that carry holiday-makers, mail and freight between Bergen and Kirkenes, tied up at Molde in the early evening. To take a car on board, there were some papers to sign and others requiring such a profusion of rubber stamp marks as only a Labour Government could devise. The process occupied the entire half-hour of the boat's stay in Molde and in the end delayed her departure by five minutes. Give a Norwegian Labour Party man a rubber stamp and he will lord it over all who need it. Even shipping companies have been affected by the disease. The procedure of loading a car onto the deck is comparable only to extracting a Christmas parcel from the post office.

It is a twelve-day round trip on these steamers to the north: I was travelling no further than Trondheim, a short overnight hop. The cruise is planned so that the places visited in daytime on the outward voyage are taken in at night on the return: every port of call is seen once in daylight. An occasional excursion is arranged ashore, sometimes between two halts, but often early in the season they are cancelled, as I learnt now, owing to the bad condition of the connecting coastal roads or the breakdown of ferries.

Certainly in fine weather it is a pleasant, unexacting vacation for elderly Americans, and particularly for retired High-school teachers, with Scandinavian forebears whose country they like to visit before they die.

# Molde

These form a good percentage of the unadventurous travellers. The rest, as I discovered a week later, are mainly from Liverpool and Leeds. It is the way to see the coast of Norway, but not Norway, to meet fellow package-tourists, but not the natives. The lure is the midnight sun, which frequently is overclouded; and there is always the boast on return that one has sailed in Arctic waters.

This was a section of the coast I had seen previously on a southern voyage. It is typical of the lovely island-studded fjord country of middle Norway. There was a call during the night at Kristiansund, that still retains its pre-war glamour with its small fishing vessels massed three or four deep, bow to stern, along the enclosed harbour, with its unspoilt timber warehouses. It is alive enough commercially not to need the tourist, and is the key to a still more beautiful hinterland.

But it was night now, and I re-pictured the place as the quayside noises broke in on my half-sleep.

For the remainder of the trip there was the long entry into Trondheimfjord. Anyone sensitive to the changing nature of fjords would know he was approaching now a different Norway from the south.

# CHAPTER 7
# TRONDHEIM AND EAST TRØNDELAG

*Although the last town towards the Pole, the traveller viewing it [Trondheim] sees nothing but what may remind him of the cities of the south. . . . There is no part of Copenhagen better built or neater in aspect than the streets of Trondheim.*

E. D. Clarke, *Travels* (1819)

Trondheimfjord cuts deep into Norway and on practical reckoning divides the north from the south, although in fact the geographical centre of the country is another five hundred kilometres further north.

Trondheim itself is best approached from the sea and is as different in character from Bergen as Bergen is from Oslo. Its natives are in a sub-category of their own: outspoken, kindly, remarkable for sustained loyalty between peaks of emotional turmoil. They can be as unpredictable as the winds that funnel suddenly through the deceptively small hills on either bank of the fjord. They are not descendants of the Vikings who came mostly from the mountainous west country; their broad fertile farmlands made it unnecessary for them to seek a livelihood abroad. Throughout history they have been a settled race of rich landowners content with life at home. They are the only people in Norway who will tell you they are busy, dismiss you and then spend two hours in sleep. Among all their fellow countrymen they are the most easily understood by Englishmen.

After Christiania had changed its name to Oslo in 1924, Tronhjem (as it was then called) became Nidaros, its name from the time of its foundation by Olav Tryggvesson in the tenth century; but while Oslo remained Oslo, Tronhjem quickly reverted to its more recent name, but in the *landsmål* form of Trondheim.

It was an elementary error of British strategy in April 1940 to pivot the defence of Norway on Trondheim. The city lies at the mercy of the surrounding hills and no army with artillery support could fail to take it. In a matter of days after the opening of the campaign the War Office plans were scrapped; no battle was fought here and the city was saved destruction. To the west are two passes into Sweden that meet at Åre across the border. The more southerly pass through Stjørdalen was used by the main body of Scottish forces of which Sinclair's regiment, destroyed at Kringen, near Otta, formed a detachment.

Trondheim's charm derives partly from its position on the peninsula formed by the fjord on one side and the river Nid on the other, partly also from its broad streets planned to contain the periodic outbreaks of fire. Although the city has been entirely or partially burnt down fifteen times, whole streets of old houses survive. The wooden wharfside emporiums on both banks of the Nid are especially colourful, but towering above all else is the largest stone building in Norway, Trondheim Cathedral.

Trondheim is the Canterbury of Norway, the cradle of Christianity, the first Archbishop's seat, and the shrine of St Olav, comparable in the middle ages to Thomas Becket's but more ancient. It is the place where all the old kings of Norway were crowned: today they are blessed there, for the ceremony of crowning has been abandoned, except for the first king of a new line.

Trondheim also channels into itself the cultural life of the north and of the surrounding districts. Many poets, painters and novelists originate in the area but commonly migrate south. It can boast of two daily newspapers, a technical college now expanding into a university, baths (Roman, Turkish and Finnish), a theatre, art school, excellent hotels, and ski slopes only ten minutes from the centre by tram. Its boiled halibut is the best in Norway.

The statue of King Olav Tryggvesson, who founded the city in 997, stands on a column in the main market square leading to the Cathedral. He is the most romantic figure in the heroic age of Norway: masterful, muscular, reputed the most handsome man of his time, with a Dublin wife, he was a celebrated person in Scandinavia before he was a candidate for the throne. Moreover, he was a champion athlete: tales are told of his feats in mountain climbing, racing, spear-throwing and skiing, or rather, running on snow-shoes. Today he would be acclaimed at the Holmenkollen international jump. At the same time he was the most unecumenical of monarchs. On becoming king he 'bade all men take up Christianity and those who spoke against it, he dealt with hard: some he slew, some he maimed and some he drove from the land'. His rough methods met with only transitory success.

Olav Tryggvesson's exploits are all recorded in the saga named after him. On his excursions overseas he harried Northumbria and Scotland, played a leading part in the critical battle of Maldon, sacked Canterbury, sanctioned the murder of Archbishop Alphege. Sailing up the Thames to London Bridge, he put ropes round the supporting piles and fastened them to his ships, which he then sailed downstream. 'When the piles were broken away, the bridge burst asunder and many men fell into the river.' The English nursery rhyme, 'London Bridge is falling down, falling down' is thought to have its origin in Olav's feat.

Always playful after victory, but gruesome in his wrath, he combined characteristics that puzzled the English; nevertheless it was in England that he accepted Christianity. On his Trondheim pillar he holds the fiery torch of his adopted religion in his left hand but, as a precaution, brandishes a sword in his right. He symbolises the reluctance of his race to commit itself irrevocably to Christianity. Vikings never burnt their boats.

Although Olav Tryggvesson built a church at Trondheim and brought over Irish clergy, Christ and the pagan gods were worshipped at times together.

Before visiting Trondheim it is well to distinguish clearly between Olav Tryggvesson and Olav Haraldsson, both kings and both associated with Trondheim. Their reigns are separated by twenty years of confused Norwegian history.

As a boy of twelve Olav Haraldsson, or St Olav, joined in the last of the Viking raids. Frequently he was in Orkney where there was a Norse plantation of pure Viking blood. At other times he was helping the

*St Olav*

English to drive out the Danes or was at the court of the Duke of Normandy. There he was converted to Christianity, then took advantage of quarrels in his native Norway to assert his rule over all the country, which he organised on the Norman feudal pattern. But there was opposition: he was irascible, uncompromising and fierce. A revolt drove him out but he returned to fight the rebel levies at Stiklestad. He was slain there in battle on 29 July 1030. At the moment of his death he became a saint.

Olav's body was taken to Trondheim, ninety kilometres to the south.

After the Reformation it remained undisturbed in its place below the altar, but in 1570 the Swedes, who desecrated the cathedral, stripped the shrine 'even to the smallest silver nail' and buried the body, along with the shrine, in a disused country church. At the end of the war, in 1571, both were returned to Trondheim with great pomp and laid in a brick-lined vault. Here Norwegians still came to pray to the saint. In 1668 the shrine was again desecrated. In an account of the remains, dating from this time, the body was described as 'rather long, well preserved, with a red beard, but the nose was somewhat sunken; the wounds inflicted on the king in his last battle were still visible; for the rest it was dry and hard as wood'.

There was nothing necessarily miraculous in the preservation of St Olav's remains. An Englishman visiting Trondheim in 1860 has a macabre account of his visit to the crypt. 'I paid another visit to the cathedral in the afternoon', he writes, 'and in a kind of vault saw a number of mummies said to be the bodies of Norwegian kings; which I doubt, for kings can scarcely be so cheap, unless they are Vikings or sea-kings. They are in rough wooden boxes and disrespectfully heaped upon each other, warehouse fashion; most of the boxes are broken, and the bodies visible. They are in an excellent state of preservation, the features being distinct and the hair remaining attached; the skin is hard and dry to the touch.'

The cathedral itself is Gothic in the English tradition. It has been restored with technical skill that has killed the inspiration of its first builders. As a reconstruction it is grand but it lacks the untampered appeal of Stavanger Cathedral, a more modest, authentic and indigenous structure.

# Trondheim and East Trøndelag

The veneration of St Olav illustrates an interesting contradiction in the Norwegian character. At the Reformation saints were put out to grass all over Norway. Devotion to St Olav, however, lingered on. A few hundred yards from the medieval cathedral across the main road leading south to Oslo, there is a miniature Catholic cathedral dedicated to the saint. It lies back from the road that follows the line of the old railway before it was diverted from the centre of the city to the waterfront. Opposite lies the large Baptist Church. Both buildings were formerly the property of the State Railways: the Catholic cathedral was the old engine shed, the Baptist church the main waiting-room, restaurant and ticket office.

In the spring sun Trondheim looked spruce, neat and clean. Visitors from the south have remarked that it would attract a larger number of visitors if it had more mould, garlic and smells. This applies equally to the Lutheran churches, well-kept, orderly and proper. They lack the odour of the ages. Trondheim Cathedral has suffered visibly from repeated spring-cleaning. At the Reformation its treasures were loaded onto two vessels that set sail for Copenhagen. One sank in the fjord and there in an unidentified spot lie the old paintings, crucifixes, plate and vestments accumulated during the five Catholic centuries since its foundation.

For months previous to my visit the papers of Trondheim and Oslo had carried almost daily reports of the goings-on of a ghost in the Cathedral. Its appearances had been noted at intervals over the last hundred years. The winter prior to my visit it had been particularly active and, in fact, had been both photographed and sculptured. Frequently it was seen in the choir dressed inexplicably in a Cistercian habit. For shortage of other copy its perambulations and guises became a feature of the national press almost as regular as the reviews of the cinema and theatre.

# Norway

Trondheim, in fact, was never a monastic cathedral, though in the province of Trondheim there had been twenty-two monasteries in Catholic times: the country to the north, rich in agricultural land, suited the monastic farmers.

On the day before my departure, the editor of the *Addressavisen*, the main Trondheim newspaper, interviewed me at the suggestion of a friend. Here, as all the way up the coast as far as Narvik, I was 'the first tourist of the year'—a label I resented since becoming a resident in Norway and subscribing monthly to the national insurance. But here was a story and I was shunted down the line to the feature editor.

Humour separates nations more than sea or mountains. The foreigner in Norway has his first pangs of exile when his jokes fall flat or he fails to laugh when he should.

I was driving north to Kirkenes before there was any certain information on the state of the roads. And I was driving back—something that had rarely been done before, since any man in his right senses would return along the good roads through Finland or Sweden. And I knew nothing about the working of a car beyond the fact that it needed occasional refuelling. What would I do in case of a breakdown? Simply open the bonnet, for this is what I had seen others do in these circumstances. And I hoped still to go on to Murmansk. All this made news.

My intention was indeed to make Murmansk. From Trondheim I wrote to the Russian Embassy in Oslo explaining that in the previous August at Helsinki I had been granted a visa for Leningrad. I was keen to go again because (I had been told) there were certain ethnical similarities between the inhabitants of the extreme north of Norway and the people over the border, and I was anxious to study them. I undertook not to stay more than four days.

I left Trondheim reluctantly. Even in the heavy rain the countryside north of the city was enchanting: there

were fine white-timbered country houses of the rich
farmers, their site, though not the structure, many
centuries old; bay succeeded bay, giving new angles of
view on to the mountains and water. The hamlet called
Hell had no interest apart from its name: the Post
Office, with its stamp mark, is a tourist attraction, and a
foreigner on returning home can ask friends whether
they had received his postcard from Hell.

Beyond Hell the country has everything Norway can
give: salmon-fishing, hunting, sailing, rich soil, forests,
open plains, broken hill terrain dominated by high
ridges. There are bears and wolves: a bear of great size
was shot here in 1967. Though so cultivated on the
surface, there are still little-known tracts of upper
Trøndelag. Besides old burial barrows, Stone Age
carvings, ruins of fortresses, there are old churches here
lying off the main road near the banks of the fjord.

Ten kilometres beyond Hell on a small peninsula

*Steinviksholm*

jutting out from the eastern bank of the fjord (I was
leaving the western side till my return) there is a
squat circular fortress built in 1525 and now under
reconstruction: a reminder of Trøndelag's forlorn
resistance to the Lutheran Reformation. Here Olav

Engelbrektsson, the last Catholic Archbishop of Trondheim (he was popular with both the citizens and peasantry), held out for nearly four weeks (24 April to 18 May 1537) against the fleet of the Danish King, Kristian III, under Eske Bille. The Archbishop escaped to the Netherlands and died the following year; Bille at an earlier meeting had presented the Archbishop with 'some water which is called *aqua vitae* and helps all kinds of humours that a man may have inside him'. Schnaps and the Lutheran religion came to Trondheim together.

Twelve kilometres short of Levanger a fat farmboy asked me for a lift into town. He had never been further south than Trondheim. I tried to adjust my ear to his dialect; he proudly pointed to his home on a hillside across a frozen lake.

Norwegians are still rooted in the country, and their sense of family, in spite of divorce and broken homes, is strong. Even in the few large towns the family adheres closely together as it does in Ireland. Outside it, there are various degrees of acquaintanceship or intimacy. Always there is a definable moment when an outsider is invited into the circle and permitted to use the singular form of address. It is not just a formality: it alters a relationship, and there is no going back on the closeness it establishes.

Levanger, the first town of any size north of Trondheim, is a pleasing centre. Here I was entertained to luncheon by the Sisters of a German secular Institute, four in all, who run an old people's home.

There are Catholic Sisters in all the principal towns of Norway. Today they are accepted everywhere with tolerance and sympathy which was markedly absent when they first entered the country more than a hundred years ago: in the town museum of Oslo there are some old paintings in which they can be seen walking in their habit down the old streets of the city. Their work is mainly among Lutherans. Here at

Levanger, in a clean, modern, efficiently-run hospital home, there was not a single Catholic; the same held of the eye hospital at Hamar. No propaganda is made among the patients who, while they appreciate that element of personal concern nuns provide the world over, appear to remain largely without understanding of the spirit of unworldliness that inspires it. At Levanger the Sisters of St Bonifacius's Institute are loved all over the town for their tender care of the aged, and on Sundays the modern church attached to their house is half-full of Lutherans, who prefer the Catholic services and pray and mix with the minute Catholic community, although in five years not one of them has taken the step of becoming a Catholic. My conviction that most Norwegians are conformists hardened: it required every-where a peculiar kind of courage not to fall in line with accepted norms of social behaviour and religious faith.

Levanger is the centre for the exploration of north Trøndelag. Here and there are remains of Viking and medieval civilisation above ground; in other places they are buried. Excavations advance slowly, mostly in summer, with the assistance of ably directed amateur archaeologists. In this way the sagas or unwritten local legends are confirmed or corrected and Norwegian history, so poor in written records, takes shape subject to continuing adjustment.

At the northern exit from the town there is a turning to the west marked Munkeby. It leads down a small valley to the head of a farm track at the bottom of which can be seen an old arch, a few unidentifiable walls, and some unkempt, crumbling and unmarked masonry. It is all that remains of a Cistercian monastery on this site.

Munkeby lies off Inndalen, the pass into Sweden that was used by Olav Haraldsson when he returned from exile in Russia to recover the kingdom of Norway. Saga, legends and folk-lore confuse the historian who wants to find out exactly what happened at Stiklestad, the battle every Norwegian child remembers when he has forgotten all the history he was taught at school. A stone church that might have been transplanted from Kent stands on the site of the old farm of Sul. On the afternoon of 27 July, 1030, Olav arrived there. Opposing his advance were all the local chieftains whose position had been undermined by his policy of centralisation and with them an immense horde of badly armed peasants. The king spent the night before the battle with Torgeir Flekk, the owner of Sul. There is an account of the battle that took place the next day, written by Grima, the old woman who nursed the wounded on the battlefield, and another by Jostein, the father of Torgeir who, though blind, walked down to the scene of the fighting to 'see' what was happening. On his return home his sight was miraculously restored. Olav himself was slain. As he threw away his sword, he would seem to have had a vision of the cross. In the measure he had understood his faith, given his upbringing and the norms of his time, he had unquestionably striven and died for the Christian cause. His death achieved what a victory could not have done. It reunited and Christianised Norway. Scenes from the battle form a frieze in the old church. On an eminence near by is a Catholic chapel, donated by Sigrid Undset, where annually on 29 July several hundred pilgrims gather to venerate the saint.

The same valley used by St Olav was the scene of a Swedish disaster in 1718, during the intermittent warfare with Norway lasting nearly a hundred years. The Swedish General Armfelt had failed to take Trondheim by siege and was forced to retreat. In mid-winter he led his army back over this pass pursued by Norwegian ski-runners. The scene described by a Norwegian captain, Emhausen, is comparable to the French army's retreat from Moscow: 'the storm lasted three days. There was no wood on the mountains. The soldiers lay dead in groups of thirty, forty, fifty or more, in full uniform, with their knapsacks on their backs; some with food in their hands or even in their mouths; the cavalry men stood on their heads in the snowdrifts as they had been thrown from their horses. Some had broken the stocks of their muskets to build a fire.'

The ski-troops responsible for the rout of the Swedes formed a special regiment based on Trondheim. An eighteenth-century English traveller described the corps as 'among the greatest curiosities of the country'. It consisted of six hundred men popularly known as the 'skaters'. Their Colonel explained how they used their 'skates': the long skate, between six and eight feet, was worn on the left leg, the other, about two feet shorter, fastened on the right, was used for pushing the longer skate forward and directing it. 'For this purpose the short skate is covered with reindeer skin, the hair of which lies smooth while the skater is progressive but bristles up and becomes rough upon any retrograde motion.' Greater speed was obtained by cutting a groove in the surface of the longer skate. The Colonel claimed that propelling themselves in this way his men could leap sometimes fifteen yards and could descend steep hills 'with a velocity swifter than any bird'. Staves were used for altering direction.

Another ten or twelve kilometres along the main road after the turning to Sweden is Maere, one of the most historic places in Norway: there is now a church there on a hillock with a view down the fjord. This had been a meeting place for the chiefs and peasants of North Trøndelag and the last heathen place of worship in the district. It is mentioned many times in the sagas. On one occasion Olav Tryggvesson sailed to Maere from Trondheim to meet the chieftains gathered for sacrifice. When they refused to be baptised, the king declared he would go into their temple to see for himself their sacrificial practices. On entering it he 'lifted up the gold-inlaid axe which he carried in his hands and struck Thor so that the image rolled down from its seat. Then the king's men turned to and threw down all the gods from their seats.' As he came out he ordered the peasants to be baptised and took hostages from them so that they would remain Christian.

If the description of the temple at Uppsala is a guide for Maere, Thor sat in the centre, with the gods Odin and Frey on either side. Thor ruled the air, controlled lightning and thunder, Odin, whose name meant madness, was the god of war, Frey (or Fred), the goddess of generation, gave peace and enjoyment.

The sacrifices, however, continued. About twenty years later, after Easter 1021, the other Olav, the saint, fitted up five ships and three hundred men at Trondheim and sailed up to Maere. He came upon the peasants at night, seized their provisions for the feast, imprisoned the chiefs, and, as the saga says, 'thus brought the whole people back to the right faith, gave them teachers and built and consecrated churches'.

The present church dates from the twelfth century; the ground enclosed by its walls is now being excavated. Among a collection of human bones beneath the floor, the base of several wooden pillars have been uncovered, the relics of a more ancient wooden church. There is a fine carved timbered ceiling, hidden at present, up a perilous staircase at the entrance to the church. It is possibly significant that many Norwegians consider the people living here in North Trøndelag today the least Christian in the country.

Between Trondheim and Levanger I had been hesitating what route to follow. There was a Catholic lady living on Leka, an island some hundred kilometres further north. The journey involved two ferries, a mountain road difficult at this time of the year and a private boat. It would take me two or three days before I was back on the main road north. My uncertainty was settled when at Levanger I learnt that the lady had left the island for a few weeks to visit friends in Trondheim.

# Trondheim and East Trøndelag

North of Levanger there was no Catholic centre before Bodø in the Arctic Circle, six hundred and eighty-three kilometres distant: the largest distance in Norway between two Catholic places of worship. On reaching Steinkjer at the head of Trondheimfjord I turned west towards Namsos.

# CHAPTER 8
# NORDLAND

*Vulgar snobs . . . and all allied genera of social im-*
*postors are snuffed out before they have spent a week in*
*Norway, and speedily return home, never to revisit the*
*land of flatbrød.*

W. M. Williams,
*Through Norway with Ladies* (1877)

Namsos, though it is part of the province of North
Trøndelag, is nearer in atmosphere to Nordland. Few
people visit it. It lies at the end of a road that branches
to the west off the main route north at Steinkjer. On the
tourist maps the Namsos road is not marked as one of
exceptional scenic beauty, but in fact it is as lovely as
any in the province. It runs first through gentle wooded
country, not unlike Østerdal, the pass lying to the east
of Gudbrandsdalen and parallel to it; then, after some
precipitous corniches, it passes above the mountain
tree-line down to lakes that are dark and lonely in the
evening.

A boy, with his satchel on his back, flagged a lift on
his way home from school. In the few hundred yards'
drive to his farm he told me he had two brothers and
two sisters. It was the first family of five I had met in
Norway: there were also five children on the neighbouring farm. This is possible only in the country.
Domestic architecture in Scandinavian cities puts large
families virtually out of the question: four children is
the limit, two or three the normal. They come fairly
soon after marriage: thirty per cent of the couples have
their first within five or six months of their wedding, and
the family is completed before the wife has reached
thirty.

Namsos was bombed to the ground on Hitler's
birthday, 20 April 1940. Seen from a distance, it is

attractive: set on the fjord level, it climbs among fir trees up the lower slopes of several small conical hills. But at close quarters it is ugly, rebuilt hastily after the war; even the new church, dominantly situated in the centre of the town, had little architectural appeal.

Here, as in all small towns I visited, was the Storgata, the Kirkegata and the Grand Hotel. Ordinarily there was no alternative to the Grand which ranges from first to sub-third class. The feature of the Namsos Grand, as of several other hotels in Norway, was that cold water flowed from the tap marked 'hot', and vice versa; but like all hotels and lodgings in Norway it was clean. A century ago no English tourist could avoid a discourse on Norwegian dirt. 'In Norway', wrote one of them (John R. Campbell), 'there is, frequently, no escape for you—you must put up in a flea-hive or bivouac out on the fjell. A tin can full of insect powder is much more to the purpose than the cart-load of eatables many travellers consider essential on a tour.'

The use of street numbers is the criterion of a town in Norway. From the number system a stranger would reasonably deduce that postmen formed the most intelligent section of the civil service. I had arranged to say Mass on the day after my arrival in the house of the single Catholic resident at Namsos. It took me two minutes to find the street and twenty to identify the house. Anyone building a house in the street appeared free to select the number he fancied provided it was not already in use, much in the same way as a young monk entering a Benedictine community chooses whatever name he pleases as long as it is not taken by one or other of his brethren.

A mere handful of people attended the Lutheran church service on the Sunday morning. It was spring. Almost the entire population of Namsos had left early for their summer huts in the hills or by the sea; in winter they spend the Sunday on skis, either following a long cross-country trail or taking off from the nearest ski-jump in preparation for the national day at Holmen-kollen. In any case, there is no tradition of regular church-going in Norway: Sunday has become the day which the family spend together either in the hills or by the sea.

*Ski-jumper*

Nevertheless the Lutheran pastor is kept busy at least with the office work put on him by the State in return for his maintenance out of public funds. He is registrar for christenings, confirmations, marriages and deaths. In Oslo there is one pastor to 9,000 members of the State Church, in the country fewer over vast areas. Some Norwegians believe that the State has increased the pastor's clerical work in order to leave him with less time for the cure of souls. There can be no doubt that this is the result.

Normally the pastor lives near the church in the *prestegård*, literally the priest's farm. At Namsos he actually lived out of town and on a farm: it was in this way he traditionally supported himself. In most parts of Norway the customary church collection is an unknown institution; there is a box for offerings at the church entrance.

Due to the small numbers in Norwegian country communities, members are distinguished by their occupation, which is used as a form of title. Thus if two persons share the same surname confusion is avoided.

# Nordland

This morning I was saying Mass in the house of Tannlege or Dentist Trygve Ingebrigtsen, whose wife was a Catholic from Glasgow. Whenever you ask the way to a friend's house, it is helpful to describe his status: Sculptor John Jacobsen, Engineer Arne Johnsen, Schoolteacher Ingrid Helgeland. Everyone knows where they live, whether they are at home, what state of health they are in. Even children give precise directions: for instance, to the second yellow house after the left fork at the top of the hill. In sending a country friend a letter of thanks for his hospitality, it is sufficient to name the person and his village. No more exact designation is possible.

During the winter the small Norwegian valleys are untouched for months by tourists. Once at Lom in February, in urgent need of a plumber, I called the telephone exchange. A game of 'happy family' followed. I asked first to speak to Mr Lund the Plumber. He was out on a job. Then to Mrs Lund, the Plumber's wife. As she was busy, I took a chance and enquired whether Miss Lund, the Plumber's daughter, was at home and told her my dilemma. The next morning Mr Lund himself hurried to the house I was occupying—the last of three in a row a hundred yards beyond a left fork a kilometre to the west of the village.

This May Sunday morning five were gathered for Mass in the living-room of Tannlege (Dentist) Ingebrigtsen. This was a true church of the diaspora. The first missionary journeys of St Paul must have had many points of resemblance to the present-day excursions of a Catholic priest in Norway.

Namsos lived mostly by timber. It was off the tourist route to north Norway. In a hard winter, when it is impossible to bring the felled logs down the mountain side, trade suffers badly. There is good trout and salmon fishing in the neighbourhood.

A road north-east from Namsos, mainly through forest, led to Grong, a junction on the route north. From Grong it took a zigzag path up a mountain gorge, then across a high plateau. As soon as it passed from Trøndelag into Nordland, there was a wildness in the scenery that distinguishes north Norway from the south. The difference is there but is hard to define: it endures to the North Cape. Cultivation is rare, habitations are more scattered, and human toil has made little impression in the centuries since Olav Tryggvesson. There is one road and the further north it gets, the more interrupted it is by ferries; to the east there are passes leading over the high mountain chain into Sweden, on the west to the coastal towns where the steamers call. In May, as the snow begins to melt, you can drive mile after mile and meet no more than the odd timber truck every half hour; there is ice still on the roads, the mountain lakes are frozen, snow clings still to the crevices of rock by the roadside. It is too early for flowers and the birch trees are scarcely in bud. There are people in the south who say that the highlands of Nordland divide a nation as well as a country; that here is a tract of the Continent that has never been Christendom. They argue that few influences that moulded the rest of Europe retained much force when they passed beyond Grong.

Some will say that there are three Norways or Norwegian types. Along the banks of the deep northern fjords, where the sun seldom penetrates and day is undistinguishable from night, the people are often unbalanced, emotional, drunk with nature, if not with alcohol. Western Norway is the home of pietism, the stronghold of sects: the people are reserved, narrow-minded but also, paradoxically, creative. In the broad fertile valleys of the south-east there is prosperity, and with it a dullness and absence of imagination.

About twelve kilometres into Nordland there was a simple hotel, mainly for fishermen, by the lake of Majavatn. The menu was unappealing with the fishballs, meat cakes and sausages to which the Norwegians remain so perversely addicted. When I asked the proprietress whether there was any fresh fish to be had, she produced two small pink trout with boiled potatoes and charged me no more than the price of the sausages.

Mosjøen, a small town of 5,000 people engaged mostly in the aluminium industry, was two hours' drive from Majavatn. Beyond Mosjøen at Mo i Rana, the geographical centre of Norway, began the ascent to Saltfjell, a high mountain plateau that was impassable in winter. There is no alternative overland route northward, except through Sweden, when the passes are negotiable. At Mosjøen I had to decide whether to continue by land or circumvent Saltfjell by sea: there was a newly-cut road from Mosjøen to the coast along the north side of Vefsnfjord to Sandnessjøen, where the steamers called.

Accurate information about Norwegian roads was still hard to get. At Namsos they said that floods had removed three hundred metres of both road and railway on Saltfjell. At Majavatn, after breakfast, the proprietress showed me an article on the front page of the local morning paper: it was an account of the first drive of the year over Saltfjell from Bodø, written in epic style. It concluded that the road was passable now provided there was no worsening in the weather. Before leaving Oslo I had heard tales of drivers on Saltfjell stopped by falls of snow and discovered dead days later in their cars.

I continued on to Mosjøen. I met no oncoming traffic, which was ominous. I had hoped perhaps here to see the royal eagle, a rare and majestic creature, in danger now of

*Royal Eagle*

becoming extinct. I had no luck. There were warnings on the road against stray reindeer that might dart suddenly from the cover of the forest across a motorist's path. None was to be seen. But at one point on this desolate plateau a small brown bear crossed leisurely across the road about fifty yards in front of me.

All through the winter the bears hibernate on a bed of moss in natural caves or in holes at the foot of the forest trees, and they emerge only in May. During this time the female produces its young. To cure their sick stomach after the winter's fast, they devour a whole anthill, which scours their inside. It is the time they attack the newly-born deer. Formerly the Lapps fought them off with spears; today they shoot them. By Norwegian law a bear that hibernates in a man's wood becomes his property. There are many tales told of bears in folk-lore: they are not fierce and attack men only if they are attacked or fear for their young. The traveller is warned not to approach any small bears he may see from his car, for usually the mother is not far off and may become enraged.

There are so few bears today in Norway that bear hunting has ceased as a sport. There are some still in the forests on the eastern border of Norway with Sweden but they have been seen also near comparatively cultivated areas in the south and west. Their normal food consists of berries, and especially bilberries, which grow luxuriantly on the moors.

The old methods of hunting bears in Østerdal are described by Malthus who toured Norway in 1799:

> The bear [is tracked] in the snow a few days before the time that he is going to lye in (as it is called). When he comes near the place where he intends to rest during the winter he goes backwards and forwards, and makes much work to prevent his being tracked—as soon as this work is perceived, the hunters take a very large cir-

cuit round, so as to be sure they have him in the ring, and mark the trees in the circle so that they may know it again. After it is supposed that the bear has been asleep two or three days, they go again and contract their former circle and so on successively till they are sure that they have him in a circle of small diameter, and having marked this they let him have his nap out till the spring; and then three or four days before his usual time of rising, go with dogs and guns. They generally see his breathing place through the snow; and sometimes kill him in his bed; at other times he gets up and runs off; but not being in a strong state, and with his feet soft and sinking a little in the snow, he cannot get on so fast as his pursuers with snow skaits and is generally overtaken and shot.

Malthus's friend, Mr Leeson, killed four or five in this manner every spring. A century later, in 1870, it was reckoned that 250 bears were killed every year. Often the carcase of a horse or cow would be deposited near the lye. The bear, hungry after hibernation, would be pounced on at its meal. Ancient books on Norway advised travellers meeting a bear to feign death and hope for the best. It is the method inculcated by folk-tales. This ruse saved the life of a youth in August 1967 in Montana's Glacier National Park, where from time to time bears surprise holiday makers.[1]

At Mosjøen, four hundred and ten kilometres from Trondheim, the question of my route was decided for me. A wild icy gale was blowing from the north, the mountain falls were heavy with melting snow, the clouds black. In all the cafés people sat in heavy outdoor winter sweaters. Only a foolhardy journalist with a high-powered car and anxious to get a story for the papers would have ventured further north.

[1] Cf. *Newsweek*, 28 August 1967, p. 16.

# Norway

The new road to the coast along Vefsnfjord was unfinished: a series of long tunnels were still being cut along the edge of what must be one of the most beautiful fjords in middle Norway. In the grim light there was every tint of grey on the waters, broken reflections of heavy clouds, a mass of shades that changed with every twist in the road. The gale emphasised the sullen temper of the fjord in May.

At the end of the road a ferry boat emerged suddenly in a cutting between two steep cliffs. I was the only passenger in the seven-minute voyage across to the island of Alsten on which lay Sandnessjøen, a fishing port with ship-breaking yards and a long wooden quay. No tourist visits it except by steamer; behind rises a seven-peaked range of mountains, the Syv Sørstre (Seven Sisters), which gives its name to the hotel and most other facilities in the place. The cinema shows films twice a week, on Tuesday and Wednesday.

The proprietor of the Syv Sørstre was so taken aback by his first visitor of the year that he personally supervised my meal. Meat, apart from reindeer in the north, is seldom up to English standards, but if there is fresh fish available it is always delectable. Fresh boiled haddock was the proprietor's recommendation and it was duly served, along with its head, tongue, liver and other entrails on a separate dish. As a treat he gave me some of his homemade *flatbrød*, a form of desiccated bread, always delicious, which keeps Norwegian menfolk perhaps the slimmest of their species in Europe.

*Flatbrød* is made from barley, rye or sometimes oats in the form of flat cakes, as thin as a wafer and about the size of a small dish. It is baked on a round iron plate or stone set on the stove and is made so quickly that it is possible to produce a year's supply in one afternoon. The bread never spoils and some prefer it when it is old: not long ago a woman was reckoned a good housewife if she produced for her son's wedding some *flatbrød* she had baked for his christening.

# Nordland

William Coxe, the English archdeacon who visited Norway at the end of the eighteenth century, has a curious footnote to his description of *flatbrød*: 'In times of scarcity they also use the bark of trees, generally of the fir; this bark is dried before the fire, ground to powder, mixed with oatmeal, baked and eaten like bread; it is bitterish and affords but little nourishment.' Mosses and lichens were also eaten, particularly the *lichen islandicus*, which was commonly used for food in Iceland.

Here at Sandnessjøen I was given also *skarke*, not a fish, but finely sliced meat that is sprinkled with salt and dried in the wind like hung beef. It is a peculiar Norwegian delicacy and requires a ploughman's stomach to digest it.

The coastal steamer, *Midnattsol*, was due to call at Sandnessjøen at 3.30 in the morning. The gale blew itself out during the night. I boarded at 4 o'clock with little fuss, for all the rubber stamps were locked up at this hour. I booked a second-class passage. As I immediately discovered, this was the way to meet the natives. The lounge was full of sprawling, yawning, half-awake, two-thirds drunk Norwegians. 'The hell of a life', remarked a young working man getting up from a table spread with dead beer-bottles. 'Why?' I asked with innocence. 'There is no service on board before 8 o'clock. Another four hours to go.' As I wanted to write up my journal, I transferred to the empty first-class lounge: I could not go on humouring a succession of drunks until the boat became alive again.

For almost the whole sea-distance between Bergen and Hammerfest the steamers sail between the coast and the endless groups of off-shore islands. On the sheltered inland side they are cultivated, seaward they are barren; a little north of Sandnessjøen many have fantastic shapes. A short sequence is particularly varied: one island stands up like the Rock of Gibraltar, another lying close by resembles pictures I have seen of Tristan da Cunha, with a high mountain sloping down to a broad verge of farming land, the next a toppling pyramid constructed to a faulty formula, yet another the backview of a hippopotamus rising from a swampy river.

Before breakfast, served at 8 o'clock, we were due to cross the line into the Arctic Circle. The Norwegian woman cleaner was busy in the saloon before the passengers were up. They are always talkative. This woman told me that I spoke Norwegian like a Finn; on a Paris metro-station I had been told I spoke French like a Russian; in Oslo a German visitor said that he understood only 'Oxford English' and could not make out a single word I said. It is difficult always in Norway to escape the views of domestics. At a house where I stayed in Oslo, the household-help, as servants are called, played bars on the piano in intervals of dusting. On discovering a Mass vestment among the clothes hanging in my wardrobe, she enquired of her employer whether I was a Cardinal. She persisted in the suspicion. It was pointless to explain that I was not even a Monsignor, a grade of ecclesiastic not unknown in Norway.

By 7 o'clock we were passing into the Arctic Circle. This was no particular excitement for me. Only nine months earlier I had spent some time in the extreme north of Finland, near Lake Inari. There, a few miles beyond Rovaniemi, there was a lot of fuss created by the tourist agency over the crossing into the Arctic: a hut with a special postmark, reindeer horns, a souvenir kiosk run by Finns in Lapp national dress.

This morning the passengers to the North Cape poured on deck as though the waters north of the Circle contained strange sea creatures not to be seen south of the line. There was sun now after the storm and it brought up onto the promenade deck white-haired American grandmothers in tight-fitting slacks, business men from Bradford armed with tinted spectacles and expensive cameras, all types but Norwegians. Mr Black and Mr Baxter were called over the tannoy; at breakfast there was the usual spread of delicious cold Norwegian dishes and all the tourists called for eggs and bacon, leaving the smoked mackerel untouched. This is a delicacy in the south, but it is always necessary to distinguish between warm and cold smoked fish. The 'cold' is almost raw, the 'warm' is processed in the same way as in England.

The coastline south of Bodø is perhaps the grandest in Norway: a series of narrow openings between high cliffs into deep fjords that run only a short distance inland and, behind, the snow-coated mountain vertebrae dividing Norway from Sweden. The grandeur lasts for hours of sailing.

There is a single call between Sandnessjøen and Bodø, at Ørnes, a village with a small hinterland of cultivation, an unspoilt place to explore. At the quay the motor

*Ørnes harbour*

launches were unloading milk from the more fertile off-shore islands. Meeting the steamer were only green-capped or -shirted girls, an indication of the scholarly ranking of the place: there were no red-caps or gymnasium graduates. Some Ørnes children doubtless went further in their education, residing for the period in

Bodø, or Mo i Rana, a hundred miles from their home.

The sun had been up since two o'clock. It seemed very late in the day when we reached Bodø, though it was only 12.30. As I was to stay here for two weeks on my return, I decided, now that my car was on board, to continue across to Lofoten, a matter of another two hours' sailing. From the outer islands I could hop by a series of ferries back on to the mainland at Narvik and so continue north to Kirkenes.

Stamsund, the most western point of the Lofoten islands, at which the steamers call, is smelt a mile out to sea before it can be seen. There is no enticement to disembark, the odour of drying fish is so overwhelming. But I had been sailing now for nearly nine hours and, though the place looked uninviting, scruples prevented me from continuing by sea. No passenger followed me down the gangway and everyone stared as though I was driving off into a trackless wilderness and would be lost to sight.

It was a relief to be rid of the steamer, impersonal, comfortable and gregarious. These passenger boats are sometimes convenient, but little more can be said for them, even if, as on the Olsen line between Oslo and Newcastle, they are equipped with saunas for those who fancy them, or with dance bands, like the theatre boat between Oslo and Copenhagen. I prefer the small miscellaneous cargo boats that go between Millwall and Oslo. It is always an excitement to be on the bridge at night as they enter Oslofjord, talk to the pilots when they are taken aboard, recognise the lights to the east and west, recollect experiences in the fjord-side towns. It costs you less, you become part of the ship's company and on a second trip you learn the troubles of the crew, that are not unlike those of an enclosed community of monks. The changes of the weather, sky and sea are instantly noticed; there is privacy and company as you are inclined. Nevertheless there are those who enjoy the steamers, several thousand a week in the season.

# Nordland

In midwinter passenger steamers are tolerable. Tourist agencies are then uninterested in them; in fact, they will tell you that they sail only from the beginning of May. This is untrue. Once, by waving an announcement in a daily paper across the desk of a travel agent, I was able to book a passage from Oslo to Kristiansand in February. There was one other passenger on board. He did not care for winter sea travel; in the summer, he told me, he could always find a young Norwegian girl who would pass the few night hours with him in a chair on deck. But for the celibate, who wants time to reflect or to write, it is a happy time to travel: in winter he has all the amenities of the boat unshared.

# CHAPTER 9
# LOFOTEN

*On Vaerøy close to Røst, there once lived a poor fisherman called Isak. He owned nothing more than a boat and a couple of goats, which he kept alive on fish offals and the few blades of grass they managed to gather on the mountains.*

Norwegian Folktale

Stamsund, on Glimsøy, is the most westerly station for the steamers calling at the Lofoten islands; south-west of it are other islands in this group stretching altogether a hundred and forty miles into the North Sea. It is yet another Norway, different from the mainland. There are wide stretches of marsh and a few scattered acres of soil sufficient for a domestic crop of potatoes, but for the most part this island consists of granite, treeless, precipitous mountains with dark fjords running into deep mysterious recesses.

In countless little ports the diminishing population lives by fishing. Between February and April in every kind of weather they put out to sea in a fleet of small motor vessels. Often they quarrel with trawlers from Grimsby or Archangel. From May to July they set their fish out to dry; they appear to rest in the late summer, then in the autumn they make their repairs for the next season. Their life revolves round the regular movement of cod and haddock that, punctually like the tide, leave the deep waters of the Atlantic in February to spawn on the banks off and between these islands. They move in compact shoals, often a hundred and fifty feet dense. A depth sounding will sometimes rest as firmly on the shoal as on the bottom of the sea.

This is perhaps the largest area of Europe that lives exclusively by the sea. There is the same pervasive stench of fish everywhere. Indoors and out it is inescapable. It comes in all winds and in still weather from the great stacks of drying cod that hang head by head on tent-like scaffolding that reaches higher than the houses. In late summer the fish are taken down and exported to Morocco, Ghana or Southern America; the roe is salted, sent to France and used as bait for sardines. The methods of the fishermen are ancient. The Vikings took fish dried in this way on their voyages to Iceland

*Fish drying in air*

and Ireland. By some old law no fish can be hung after 12 April or removed before 12 June.

In May the guano factories for grinding fish heads and offal into powdered fertilisers add to the stench, and there are fumes also from the boilers extracting oil from cod livers.

# Norway

*Tran* is the Norwegian name for cod liver oil. The new foreign resident is told that if he dispenses with it in winter he will find his sight failing, his strength sapped before noon, his hair or teeth falling out; that there is no vitamin to substitute for it. A liqueur glassful a day is mercifully sufficient: if the oil is stale, it is doubly undrinkable.

Here, but also in all places in Norway, the visitor must be prepared for fish balls and fish pudding. Both are made by pounding raw fish in a mortar with eggs, flour, milk or cream: the paste or pulp thus produced is fried or boiled into flat or rounded cakes. When properly made it can be very good; but shop-produced, it is tasteless.

At the seaman's hostel in Stamsund I got a bed with difficulty. There was no fish to be had in the café, only *lapskaus*, a kind of stew that is eaten at least once a week in every Norwegian household. Made with passable meat by a skilful *husmor* and washed down with aquavit and beer, it is a good dish but, like fish pudding, it is to be shunned in small restaurants. Here it consisted of old sausages stewed with potatoes, a glutinous and inedible substance at which I could no more than nibble.

By the end of the evening the hostel had filled with naval and air force officers. There was activity in the streets until the early morning. As I was to learn, the further north you get, the later the population retires: in the extreme north it is awake all night.

The Lofoten islands attract many journalists, but mainly in the cod season. Before I left Stamsund the next morning a fisherman, with an expression of intense sympathy in his eyes, asked me whether I was married. When I showed surprise at his question, he explained that he thought I was the Englishman whose wife had died at sea—her body had been brought to Stamsund and was being buried that morning. Even today the loss of life in these waters is considerable. On one of the outer islands there is a graveyard with names only of women on the headstones—all the menfolk lost their lives at sea. The fishermen of Lofoten are religious when they are about their work; on land they are God-fearing, but not church-goers. A few belong to a curious sect found only here. For no logical reason they believe that the second coming of Christ will occur in Lofoten in the year A.D. 4000, but since adherents of the sect marry only among themselves, they are likely to be extinct before the event.

Already extinct is another peculiarity of the islands, the *lofothest* or Lofoten horse. The last specimen of this

*Lofoten horse
from Bergen Museum*

species, which is said to have been common in most parts of prehistoric Europe, died in Lofoten in the last century and is now to be seen stuffed in the Bergen museum. It is short and shaggy, not unlike the Shetland pony.

Alongside the fishermen's houses cats were prowling under the desiccated cod strung like socks on a clothes-line. The ribs of the scaffolding stood out against the wet grey sky like the concrete poles of a half-completed cathedral. At every fishing quay the bare mountains came sheer down to the shore.

It is the combination of bleakness with beauty that explains the seduction of Lofoten, a world apart from the rest of Europe that entices the lonely traveller to return. There is little growth on this island, just a few mountain sheep, innumerable inlets and variations in the groups of skerries in succeeding bays. Every turning of the earth-surfaced road seems to hold an individual unrepeated beauty, a private region for the wanderer to explore.

At the southern end of the island to the south, off Lofotodden, is the maelstrom. In winter it is wild and dangerous but barely noticeable in calm summer weather. Its cause is evident, for the sea, in places more than 150 fathoms to the west of the islands, pours between two of the group through a channel not more than 30 fathoms. In stormy weather the turmoil is treacherous. The waters coursing round the outer circle in a diminishing sweep suck into the gulf any man, boat or beast not powerful enough to keep its course.

In calm weather there is so little trace of the whirlpool that some tourists find difficulty in believing that it exists. It is mentioned first in Hakluyt's voyages: 'There is [he says] between the said Røst islands and Lofoten a whirlpool called Malestrand which makes such a terrible noise that it shaketh the rings in the doors of the inhabitants' houses of the said islands ten miles off.' The eighteenth-century writer, Erik Pontoppidan, describes how frequently whales, coming near to the maelstrom, were swept into it, howling and bellowing in their struggle to escape. 'A bear once attempting to swim from Lofotodden to Mosken, with a design of preying on the sheep at pasture in the island, afforded the like spectacle to the people; the stream caught him and bore him down, whilst he roared terribly, so as to be heard on shore.' The word which gave the title, *A Descent into the Maelstrom*, to Poe's book is one of the few, like 'ski', that Norway has given to other countries: all without exception concern natural phenomena or outdoor activity.

An Italian sea-captain, Quirini, wrecked in the North Sea in 1432, came ashore on an island of the Røst group.

# Lofoten

The account of his adventures contains the only description of life in north Norway in the Middle Ages.
The island was three miles in circumference. Quirini counted 126 inhabitants. They grew neither fruit nor grain, but as today they salted and dried their catch of cod and haddock, and in May took it by sea to Bergen. This was their main diet but, says Quirini, they also pounded their dried fish until it became tender and then mixed it with batter and spices to form a substance similar to a modern Norwegian fish pudding. Their drink was sour milk. Quirini, who disliked it, was given beer. He says their houses were made of timber, but circular in shape with an opening for light in the roof, which was covered with a translucent membrane in winter. Their clothes were made of coarse London cloth imported from Bergen. Geese and other birds were tame; the islanders, when they needed eggs, lifted the geese from their nests, then settled them in again.

Little has changed since the fifteenth century, though moral behaviour may have declined. Quirini gives an idyllic description of their 'perfect observance of the moral law'. They never barred or bolted any possessions or property. They attended church regularly and observed all the fast days.

Before Quirini left Røst in May, he received from the Governor's wife a gift of sixty dried codfish.

On his way south he met Ålsak Bolt, the Archbishop of Trondheim, and on the feast of the Ascension attended Mass in the cathedral where he saw a white bear skin about fifteen feet in length. Then on a horse given him by the Archbishop he proceeded overland into Sweden. Everywhere in Norway he had experienced open hospitality. The countryside was even more thinly populated than now. With his guide and companions he would come late at night to open farmsteads where all were asleep. The party would take a meal and stretch out for the night under ticks filled with down.

In the morning the householder showed no surprise at finding them there. Quirini remarked on the huge mountains and deep valleys and on the large number of animals that resembled roebucks. He also saw snow-covered white birds he had not seen in Italy.

My destination was Svolvaer on the neighbouring island of Austvågøy. But I was reluctant to leave the fantastic wilderness of the island I had discovered. At a petrol station I had enquired the distance to the ferry at Smorten. It was four kilometres and I had five minutes on the rough twisty road to reach it. I could not face another meal of Stamsund *lapskaus*.

Norwegians always underestimate distances just as people in small countries always exaggerate them. It is wise for the motorist to add at least half again to the distance he is told: and to be wary when the estimate is given in miles. A Norwegian mile is ten kilometres. Over terrain like the Lofoten islands ten 'miles' is a good day's journey.

There is a useful sheet, obtainable from tourist offices, giving the times of the principal Norwegian ferries on the routes in west and north Norway. But ferries are innumerable and multiply every year. To be informed on all, it is necessary to carry about a book the size of a London telephone directory. Generally when you confront suddenly an oncoming stream of five or six cars on a lonely road, it is a sign that the ferry has pulled in. Similarly, if cars frantically overtake you at high speeds, you also must hurry: the ferry is about to sail. There may not be another for two or six hours. It may be the last that day. In Lofoten, where the people are particularly kind, ferry boats a few hundred yards out from the pier will return to the quay in answer to a prolonged hoot. This happened as my car appeared down the final slope to the shore.

The clouds came down almost to the base of the mountains as the ferry from Smorten chugged across to Lyngvaer on Austvågøy, where Svolvaer lay. It was as

# Lofoten

though the next island in the group was veiling its secrets. How high did these mountains rise? Suddenly, after half an hour at sea, the sun broke through and the pier at Lyngvaer could be seen just a hundred yards away. Austvågøy was grand, but in a less rugged way than Vestvågøy. I was approaching Svolvaer, its capital, from the south-east. It is the north-west of these islands that are loveliest: there are bays remembered for life that distil an enchantment no photograph can catch. On the hill above the quay the road took a bend down a long precipice and revealed a world within a world: vegetation but no trees, marsh replacing rock, more smoothly rounded skerries, colours that seemed less foreboding in the sun that now broke in shafts through the dark clouds.

Svolvaer, lying in a sheltered bay backed by steep mountains, each with a name that added character to the place, was spoilt by massive petrol containers, a cruel indication that the fishing industry was capitalised. After watching a silly American film in the early evening I visited H. J. Bjørnstad, an Advokat: there were two Advokats in the town, their office corresponding roughly to a solicitor's in England. His house stood back from the road, overlooking a small inlet of the Svolvaer sound. Like all Norwegian homes it appeared from outside much smaller than in fact it was: even mountain or seaside 'huts' have more rooms than ever looks possible from the exterior. Little space is ever wasted on a hall, the staircase usually being brought down into the *stua* or living-room.

By dignity of rank Bjørnstad was the principal citizen of Svolvaer. My visit was unannounced; his wife was out for the evening, his two daughters occupied with their home-work after their *middag*. Bjørnstad's study was lined from floor to ceiling with works of literature, reference, law and history. Courteously he answered my enquiries on the Lofoten islands; he recommended me books, offered to reply by letter to any further questions I might have. There were sad facts he gave me about the fishing industry. Formerly 150 million kilograms of fish were caught in a good year, now only 20 or 40 million. In Bjørnstad's youth there were 20,000 fishermen on the islands, now no more than five or six thousand. The future was uncertain.

Advokat Bjørnstad could laugh at the vagaries of the people of Svolvaer: he was their counsellor, solicitor and friend. Recently a young married woman of twenty-eight had come to him seeking a divorce—a transaction arranged in Norway between lawyers. The reason she gave was that her husband had begun to bore her after five years of married life: she wanted to try another. The Advokat advised them to separate for three months. They did this, reunited and were now living happily together again.

Bjørnstad spoke of the British raid on the Lofoten islands on 4 March 1942 as though it had occurred yesterday. When the troops landed at 5 o'clock in the morning, the islanders thought the operation was part of a Continental invasion. The raiders left the same evening. Within a few days the S.S. troops were in Svolvaer. Reprisals were made, and, in response, the Norwegian resistance took shape. Several hundred Lofoten islanders, however, were taken to Scotland, along with papers snatched from the office of the German harbour-master in Svolvaer. There was a simultaneous swoop on Stamsund and two other fishing harbours.

At a later stage in our conversation I noticed on the walls of the Advokat's study a fine painting of a young girl by the Lofoten artist, Gunnar Berg. This was the beginning of the second part of the evening. It was now past ten o'clock.

Gunnar Berg had died in 1893 at the age of thirty. His house, now occupied by his nephew, was a short distance along the road I had taken from the ferry quay. The Advokat immediately telephoned and we were invited to visit the house, where Mr Berg had a collection of his uncle's paintings. It was raining heavily now. As I had drunk some brandy and soda, I was disqualified from driving. Another phone call, and Berg offered to fetch us. 'So now we can have another drink', said the Advokat.

There was something unusual about the Bergs' home that I instantly appreciated but could not identify. I was still puzzled when Mr Berg pointed out that his house, a little back from a mountain stream that ran down through his property into the fjord, was set in a thick plantation of trees.

Mr Berg's father, the brother of the painter, had resolved to disprove the accepted belief that no trees grew in the Lofoten islands. He had imported several dozen firs, and after they had taken root, introduced mountain ash, pine and other European trees and, finally, some Japanese and eastern ones—in all about sixteen different kinds. At the age of eighty he had planted another four hundred fir saplings, which now formed a thick copse on the hillside. A faded photo in the living-room showed the house when the property was treeless: it looked like the rest I had seen; now, in the late evening sunshine, it seemed transported from another region of the world.

Mrs Berg asked me when I had last eaten. In a few minutes she had brought out the most delicious smoked salmon I had tasted in any country: it was the first to be caught in Svolvaer that year. Then she explained: caught on Friday, smoked over the week-end, eaten on Wednesday, that was how it should be treated. A smoking plant was pointed out to me across the garden. In August, when there were trout in the stream outside his living-room, Mr Berg caught sometimes two or three in the evening, sometimes thirteen on a good day. He could cast his line from the window and to preserve his catch for other days he had built this small smoking plant. In a country as long as Norway the fishing season varies a great deal between south and north, the coast and the high mountains. The best time anywhere is said to be when the birch leaves are the size of a mouse's ear. This allows for more than eight weeks' difference between Oslo and Lofoten.

Berg's uncle, like many Norwegian painters in the last century, had lived mostly in Dusseldorf, Paris, and Berlin, where he is mainly represented today, but there was a collection of some fifteen smaller paintings in this house: realistic, exact, and inspired by the bleak grandeur of Lofoten. One canvas showed a funeral procession to a cemetery near this spot: the coffin was being drawn on a sleigh over a snow-field to the graveyard. In a hard winter, Mr Berg explained, it was the custom to leave the coffin under the snow until the spring thaw had softened the ground sufficiently for a pit to be dug.

A law in Viking days prohibited alcohol at sea. In the Lofoten islands wine could be had but not spirits. The restrictions in hotels baffle and infuriate tourists: they vary from place to place and, according to holidays, from week to week. Further south I had struck a long stretch of days on which not even wine could be bought: the State-controlled shops were closed on Saturday and Sunday and again on Monday, for it was the eve of National Day, 17 May; they were closed again on the 17th itself and on the day after, the eve of the Ascension, and on the Ascension itself. At Svolvaer the Commune was now applying for a licence to sell spirits: a Storting committee was sitting on a revision of the law. In certain narrowly evangelical areas of western Norway the puritanical vote against drink of any kind makes the whole commune forcibly dry.

Nevertheless Mr Berg offered me cognac with coffee before we parted. He explained that it had to be fetched from Bodø, three hours' sailing from Svolvaer.

It was well after midnight when Advokat Bjørnstad took me back to his house: he insisted on my waiting for his wife's return and having a drink with her. I knew now that I was in a world where the distinction between day and night was determined by the individual. Unless a man is tied by business, he pleases himself how he divides the twenty-four hours of summer sunlight. It is the same all the way to the North Cape: a land in which trees, flowers and shrubs grow without pause, and canaries are covered in their cages so that they do not sing themselves to death. Hakluyt writes of this land in his account of Chancellor's voyage to Russia in 1553: 'He came at last to a place where he found no night at all, but a continual light and brightness of the sun shining clearly upon the huge and mighty ocean.' When people further to the south are asleep, here they are gossiping or doing business in the street. On Sunday mornings not a child is astir before midday. To the casual visitor it is a mad world that quickly becomes the norm. In the *Vinland Saga* the Vikings located the places they discovered in the north by measuring the difference between day and night. There is a word, *døgnavild*, used in the north, especially in relation to Lapps: it denotes a sickness, diagnosable as any other, which afflicts northerners and makes them incapable of distinguishing day from night, morning from evening. The medieval Popes were alert to this and dispensed Catholics in north Norway from the obligation of fasting from midnight before taking Communion. Further south, where people were dependent on their catch of fish, there was no duty to attend Sunday Mass if a shoal of brisling was reported that day in the fjord.

At 2 o'clock by my watch I drove back to my hotel, drew my curtains and read by the outside light. Only by reasoning with myself did I know that it was night. The legend that these northern Norwegians did not go to bed in summer was not an exaggeration after all.

At the north-east point of this island, about 20 kilometres from Svolvaer, a ferry was marked at Fiskebøl over to Hadseløy, the island on which Stokmarknes, a large shipbuilding centre, was situated. I had plotted a route from there, across the outer ring of islands, to Harstad. This morning only road-makers were to be seen, ubiquitously active in all weathers during the summer months throughout the north. As I continued along the rocky fringe of the fjord, they looked at me with increasing curiosity; when I arrived at Fiskebøl I realised that I had read my map carelessly: the ferry was marked to open this year and was not yet in operation.

The only way to get away from Svolvaer was by boat to Skutvik on the east side of Vestfjorden, the strait running between Lofoten and the off-shore group of islands. From Stutvik, using two more ferries, I could reach Harstad.

For most of mankind there is nothing to do in a small Norwegian town: in season there is fishing or skiing, between seasons only sleeping or sitting. Back in Svolvaer, with the greater part of the day on my hands, I visited the town hall for want of something better to do. It occupied the top floor of a municipal block: on the street level there were shops, offices and the cinema I had attended the previous afternoon. In the main assembly room of the Commune was a large canvas by Berg, his only work on semi-public view. It depicted in Victorian detail and exactness a battle between two warring groups of Lofoten fishermen in Trollfjorden near which I had just passed. A long legend below explained every detail of the painting. In fact, in every fjord and fishing harbour, from Reine that lies south of Stamsund to the northernmost tip of the islands there was a story of disaster or battle to be gathered.

That evening the vibration of the engines prevented me writing my journal on the long sea-crossing to Skutvik. But I had the *Vinland Saga* with me: the two hours in the straits were sufficient to read and annotate it. I thought that the treeless Lofoten islands must resemble Iceland: how else explain why these Vikings transported timber from Newfoundland to their home settlements? How like them were the present occupants

of Lofoten: they appreciated the same type of good
looks, they still gaped with their eyes, mouth and
nostrils looking up to the sky, they lived still 'on game
from the mainland, eggs from the islands and fish from
the ocean'; they knew their sea creatures. How ill a
Viking party became after eating an unidentified species

*Reine in Lofoten*

of whale washed up on the coast. Once convinced that
Christianity was better than their old gods, there was
nothing to curb their evangelising zeal: on an expedition across the north Atlantic they captured, forcibly
baptised and loaded onto their long ship two Red
Indian children, the first American Christians. Their
spirit has been inherited by the Norwegian State
Church which is productive of missionaries in most
corners of the world.

There was an inn at Skutvik. After midnight the
proprietress was at the door, ready with the welcome
that seamen received in Viking days on their return
home. The smell of fish was there also; it kept me awake
with the virulence of a nightmare.

# CHAPTER 10
# HARSTAD-NARVIK-TROMSØ

*The Lapps are so called because they are foolish people of little intelligence, quite savage and in some ways like animals. No civilized nation has any communication with them.*

Sebastian Munster, *Cosmography* (1544)

Between Skutvik and Harstad there were two ferries connecting the road that ran for the most part through gentler country along the east side of Vestfjorden. At Bognes there was a boat to Lødingen which gave me time for further reading in the Sagas.

*Njål's Saga* was full of murder, brutal love-making, trials of arms. An evil demon seems to have possessed the Norwegians when they settled in Iceland. Some writers explain it, probably rightly, by pointing out that the men troublesome at home were driven to find a new livelihood there. Long after the island had become Christian *Njål's Saga* recounts an endless series of deeds of calculated vengeance, rightfully exacted, precisely planned and executed in frigid hatred. Iceland of the twelfth century was perhaps a rough equivalent of Botany Bay in the reign of George III, but British criminals had a kinder code of conduct.

Harstad, on the largest of all the Norwegian islands, is an old town, the visible limit of Christian influence in the Norwegian north during the Middle Ages: there is written evidence of churches further north, but none remain. Here, or rather at Trondenes, three miles away, is the most northerly medieval church in the world, well sited, built in stone, with some faint surviving features of interest. Beyond this point there is nothing left of what the Norwegians designate as Catholic times.

But the church is symbolic also, for it was built by King Håkon Håkonsson (1240–63), whose reign marks the beginning of the greatest period in Norwegian history, which lasted to the Black Death. The builder is known, also the priest, Audun Rande, who later became Bishop of Iceland: many of the old churches there date from his episcopate. Its position on a promontory made

*Trondenes church*

it also a defence post against the Finlanders, who raided this part of Norway in the thirteenth century. Round the present church it is possible to trace defence works, as high as fifteen feet in parts.

Frequently Lapps encamp on the outskirts of the town, always in their national dress. When the tourist steamers hove in sight they come down to the quay with their knives, baskets, belts, snow-shoes and other wares for sale. The snow-shoes are lined with a coarse grass that must be renewed every year: this accounts for their warmth. But they are made for use on the hard snows of the north; in the south there are perhaps four weeks in the average winter when they can be worn.

Harstad is off the main overland route north, on the periphery of European culture, but commercially thriving; it is the centre also of the military section of the Norwegian defence forces. The commanding officer was General Paul Magnus Strande, a gay, slim, upstanding, efficient soldier, who spoke crisp English with an easy command of technical words. In the 1940 campaign he had fought as a young lieutenant, had been imprisoned, released and had taken a job in the Ministry of Religion and Culture. But soldiering was in his blood; he escaped to the Shetlands, a forty-eight hour crossing in a trawler. Later, he explained, there was a regular ferry service between Scotland and the secret departure quays in the Norwegian fjords, with over seventy points of wireless contact between the two countries. In 1944 he was back in Norway on a resistance job. His story was very similar to others told me by high-ranking army men.

Harstad appeared crowded: the streets, church, quay-side and hotels had been taken over by an influx of 'Lions', a body corresponding to the Rotarians, for their annual convention. The General had to make a speech at the banquet: he regretted that he could not take me to meet his wife and share their *middag*.

Frequently in midsummer but rarely at other times, the visitor to Norway finds all hotel accommodation booked by these conventions. Now there were also preparations for a theatre festival. Harstad was determined to assert itself culturally.

In the Lofoten islands there had been continuous and clear daylight. Here for the first time (it was 28 May) I saw the midnight sun, its orb swollen, spreading a golden haze over the skerries in the fjord. Later, further north, it varied in glory with the altering atmosphere and season of the year. The first sight of it made me wonder what precisely David had in mind when he wrote: *nox sicut dies illuminabitur*, the night shall be lit up like the day, for the phrase summed up an experience he surely never had. In winter, of course, these places are mostly in darkness. The people here find the succession of lightless days hard to endure: exertion, mental or physical, is minimal then. Speak to any Norwegian between Harstad and the North Cape and he will tell, without hesitating a moment, the month and the day when the sun first strikes the mountain peaks, and when it comes down into his valley. There it stays for the period that is reckoned summer, which begins and ends with the precision of a timetable.

*Midnight sun*

Narvik is a town with little history of its own, but is embedded in the epic of the British Navy. Planned in 1892, it came into being in 1902 and provided an ice-free port for the shipment of iron ore from the Swedish frontier only twenty-five kilometres away. It was to deny the Germans this ore that the Allies attempted to hold it in 1940.

The approach from Harstad over the ferry at Steinsland follows the north side of Narvik fjord. The road runs alongside high mountains through a constantly changing countryside; in the small inlets of the fjord the German destroyers lurked unnoticed in April 1940 when Captain Wharburton-Lee with brilliant seamanship led in his British squadron to occupy Narvik. It was the first place won and the last relinquished in the ill-prepared campaign. The war cemetery at the northern exit from the town epitomises the story: there are graves of Polish airmen, French Chasseurs Alpines, British sailors 'known only to God', and the flat, square, grey, granite slabs of the Germans. The older generation in Narvik had clear memories of the May days when there was no shelter of darkness for the advancing destroyers. One man on the south side of the fjord pointed out the spot where *H.M.S. Hardy* was beached and the school where her survivors were billeted, another could remember how the entire population of a certain valley remained drunk for days on the supplies of liquor left behind by the Allies.

The war museum is a gruesome effort to offer a morsel of interest to the tourist: the plans of the battles are well made, but the exhibits are horrific.

It was Whit Sunday evening when I arrived. Inevitably I stayed at the Grand Hotel. In the dining-room three young Norwegian married couples sat in total silence eating their *middag*. For the space of an hour not a word was exchanged among them all; and nothing was said to the waitress, for they were making their way through the set meal. I had seen this uninterrupted silence often enough in Finland, even among youths in cafés: perhaps it was the way of all the people in the north.

Here in the military cemetery lay the bones of a young Lieutenant of the Chasseurs Alpines, Xavier Rénom de la Baume, killed in the retreat from Namsos in which his regiment, the only Allied unit properly equipped for winter fighting in Norway, had formed the rearguard. De la Baume was a Jesuit, conscripted in the French army in 1939.

By Article One of the 1814 Norwegian Constitution, Jesuits, Monks and Jews were excluded from the kingdom. Gradually a more liberal view of non-Lutherans prevailed, thanks chiefly to the romantic poet, Henrik Wergeland. First, in 1851, Jews were admitted, then in 1897 the monastic orders and, finally, in 1956 by a vote of 111 against 31, Jesuits. Curiously the Christian People's Party, who drew their support mainly from the western valleys, voted to a man against this most recent change in the Constitution. In the heated debate on the Jesuit issue in the Storting, it was pointed out that, after the war, when there was the question of removing his remains to France, the priest's father, the Comte de la Baume, preferred that they should stay in Narvik in the hope that some day the Norwegians would repeal their proscription on the Order to which he belonged. Switzerland is the only European nation that today maintains its ban on the Order.

At the hotel desk I asked whether it could be arranged for me to say Mass the next day in the chapel of the war cemetery. 'Today is Palm Sunday', was the reply, 'And tomorrow is a holiday'. 'Whit Sunday . . . today', I corrected the clerk. 'Oh, I don't care what day it is', he answered me, 'Tomorrow is a holiday and that's all that matters.'

The hotel bar was closed for the same reason as the cemetery chapel. Outside, in the city square, was a grotesque black statue of a muscular Norwegian woman with an infant astride her right arm: a fine physical specimen that registered every sinew in her torso. It was anyone's guess why she was there and what she represented. When it comes to sculpture Norwegians have a knack of offering the foreigner a gross outsized image of themselves.

Centuries have rooted religious prejudices deep in the Norwegian mind. Even today the school text-books teach that Jesuits hold unmentionable moral precepts. In discussion on boats, trains and in family circles I have come across the immovable conviction that Jesuits make progress by international intrigue, defend regicide and incendiarism, maintain that the end justifies the means, that lying, as with the ancient Greeks, is a question of skill, not of morals. Ship-chandlers, foresters and fishmongers, at one time or another, have tried to explain to me what Jesuits hold on equivocation. The chandler, who had recently read *Macbeth* at school, was certain he was better informed than myself on the Jesuit, Henry Garnet, whose biography I had written. Even among students in the University theological faculty, these beliefs linger. Once in such an audience I claimed that in the innumerable writings of the Jesuits and in their archives seized a dozen times by revolutionary governments all over Europe, no support could be found for these mouldy libels. Even if this statement of mine was true, asked a student, did not the Jesuits take a secret oath not to reveal their own teaching? I could only answer that in no other case, then, had so many secrets been kept by scores of thousands of men for a period of four hundred years.

Over the long toll bridge north of Narvik the road zigzags steeply up the flank of a mountain onto a high plateau. Two German and one Swedish car overtook me, the first tourists I had met since leaving Oslo. Driving south two months later on the same road, tourist cars came like locusts: first singly, then in small numbers, finally in crowds no one could count. These early motorists were wise to choose this time, before the buds had scarcely formed on the mountain ash and birch. In another six weeks the thick foliage on the fringes of the road would screen from view the panorama of the mountain peaks: now it was open for miles on all sides.

Even in the north, at intervals on the main artery, or slightly off it, there are mountain hotels: in the south they are more common. They are a feature of both Norway and Sweden, in a category and with a character of their own. Usually they are sited on remote mountain *viddas*: they can be enclaves of comfort, sometimes of luxury, in wild country; centres for skiing, mountaineering, leisure, fishing or reflection. Their atmosphere is always friendly, on a second visit even intimate, and for a protracted stay, the charges are reasonable. At Christmas they provide festal days for single people; at Easter bookings are heavy and made months in advance. There was such an hotel at Gratangen about 35 kilometres from Narvik, built high above an inlet of Astafjord and unfrequented at this season of the year. At the reception desk sat a young Norwegian girl in country dress knitting a sweater—they all do it. The sweaters have complex and infinitely varied patterns, with shades that vary with the district; they are warmer than an electrically heated jacket, last more than a lifteime, in fact, are handed down from mother to daughter. It is the same with stockings, mittens and bonnets. Certain designs are special to districts in the

*Norwegian knitted cap, mittens and stocking*

south, but as a cottage industry knitting has survived universally. Occasionally the taste is garish, but this holds also for the modern Norwegian painted furniture which cannot be compared in delicacy of colouring with the eighteenth-century work.

Bardufoss, about half way between Narvik and Tromsø, is a key military base. For a stretch of ten miles the road was tarred: then the rough, pitted, broken natural surface continued. Approaching Balsfjord at a roadside resthouse I encountered my first Lapps, man and wife, squat, broad-faced, ruddy complexioned, with heavy lower lip and fleshy flat nose turned up at the tip; both had brown eyes, the man a sparse beard and coarse hair. By western standards they were not good-looking. The couple were talking animatedly over coffee and buns. They looked strong and visibly toughened by the climate. The man carried an ornamental belt and, hanging from it, a knife in a finely carved sheath. Across the room three Norwegian youths sat in total silence. I knew now that they said nothing because they had nothing to say: nothing happens in the north.

The first author to mention the Lapp people was Tacitus in his *Germania*, in the second century. Succinctly he retailed the reports he had heard of these 'barbarians': they did not cultivate the land, they ate only what grew wild, they slept on the bare ground. Men and women hunted together; their only protection against the weather was a primitive hut made of staves.

The next reference to them is four centuries later, in the Byzantine historian Prokopios. His details are good reporting. The Lapps, he had been told, dressed in skins and lived almost like animals. Among them a mother was never known to suckle her infant: she put a morsel of marrow in its mouth, then wrapped it in a pelt which she hung from a branch of a forest tree.

Oddly, the earliest first-hand account of the Lapps occurs in English literature. It was given by Ottar, a Norwegian from Hålogaland, on a visit to Alfred the Great, who transcribed it into his Saxon edition of Orosius's *World History*.

The Lapps that I was to meet later understood and spoke Norwegian: among themselves they spoke Samish, which resembles Finnish. The correct name for them is Samé: Lapp is a pejorative word meaning 'fool'. They spread over the northern stretches of four countries: 20,000 in Norway, 10,000 in Sweden, 3,000 in Finland, and perhaps 2,000 in Russia.

At Vollan, at the head of Balsfjord, the road forks north to Alta and west to Tromsø, the capital of the province of Troms. Tromsø is on a humped island over which tower high mountains on the outer approaches from the sea. Its situation fits it for the role of supremacy among the northern cities. In recent years it has been connected with the mainland by the longest suspension bridge in Norway; it has an airport and a cable lift to a mountain summit which gives what must be one of the grandest scenic views of Europe. Norwegians here claim that it is the Paris of the north, but its non-scenic attractions can be exhausted in a short afternoon. Soon it will have a university.

Tromsø lies off the main overland route north and for this reason it escaped destruction at the end of the war: there are streets of wooden buildings surviving intact from the mid-nineteenth century. It is the see of a Lutheran and a Catholic bishop.

On the site of the Lutheran cathedral above the harbour in the main street King Håkon Håkonsson built a church about 1250 and 'Christianised the whole parish'. The church was planned as a centre for missionary work among the Lapps, but this was never undertaken. Håkon's church was known as *Mariakirke iuxta paganos*, Mary's church close by the pagans.

An optimism similar to King Håkon's infected the Catholic missionaries six centuries later. My host at Tromsø was John Wember, the Catholic bishop of northern Norway. He showed me an ecclesiastical map of this area, drawn by the Roman officials and printed, of all places, in Glasgow in 1865. It gave the boundaries of what was grandly designated as the Prefecture Apostolic of the North Pole. The text was in French.

The jurisdiction included everything above the 60th meridian, with a loop to the south that embraced the Faroes, Orkney, the Shetlands, South Greenland and Caithness. Missionary stations were marked at Kirkwall, Lerwick, Kirkeboe in the Faroes and Wick; there were another three in Iceland at Reykjavik, Holmar and Skalhott, one in South Greenland at Gård, nothing in north Canada or in New Galloway or Cumberland Island. Only Troms and Finnmark, along with Spitz-bergen and Bear Island, are now under the jurisdiction of the Catholic Bishop in north Norway. The map remained a chimera of a Roman ecclesiastical carto-grapher.

An English visitor to Tromsø in 1876 was alarmed to find the Hotel du Nord, then the only hotel in the town, run by a 'semi-French woman, a Roman Catholic' placed there by the Catholic mission to whom the hotel belonged. Though well treated, W. M. Williams, in his book *Through Norway with Ladies*, reflected with some prejudice: 'In thus securing the only hotel, the Mission probably calculates upon obtaining considerable in-fluence, but has not succeeded. There are scarcely any people in the world less likely to be won back to Romanism than the Norwegians. A commercial associa-tion for the cultivation and sale of water melons would have about the same prospects of success in Arctic Norway as a Jesuit propaganda.' To his relief, Williams found the Hotel du Nord burnt to the ground on his return from the North Cape a week later. It is now, of course, replaced by the Grand, which has no Romanist links.

Tromsø's interest is its association with the expedi-tions to the Arctic; there are statues of Nansen and Amundsen, a fine Arctic museum, and for the tourist who wants trophies without perils, the pelts of ice-bears (as they call the polar bear) to be had for £150. Reindeer skins cost only £5 but they are liable to moult.

Certainly here the people suffered from *døgnavild* or this northern inability to distinguish between day and night. After retiring late on Saturday evening I woke with a start, believing I had overslept: I was due to say an early Mass on Sunday morning. My watch had stopped shortly after 1 a.m. It was as bright as day, commune officials with pneumatic drills were busy repairing a burst water main, a ship hooted in the

# Tromsø

sound, crowds of young people were talking loudly above the rasping of the drill, the main street was full of excited children, bands were playing. I dressed hastily, went out to check the time by a street clock, to find that it was only two-thirty. Later in the morning there was scarcely a soul astir before midday. Habits have changed little here. More than a hundred and forty years ago the English traveller, E. D. Clarke, observed the same as I had done at Tromsø. 'The lower order of people in summer,' he wrote, 'sit up the whole night and take no sleep for a considerable length of time. Sunday, in fact, is their sleeping day: if they do not go to church, they spend the greater part of the sabbath in sleep; and in winter they amply repay themselves for any privation of their hours of repose during summer.'

An advantage in travelling so early in the year (this was the first week-end of June) is that the salmon travel north with you. Here, as in Svolvaer, I was treated to the first salmon caught this year in the fjord.

Tromsø is the capital of the Norwegian Arctic. Here on 7 June 1940 King Håkon and his Government boarded the cruiser *Devonshire* and crossed to England to continue the fight against Germany: about half the Norwegian merchant fleet was sunk on convoy work with the loss of 4,000 seamen. On the outskirts of the town is a modern museum, which epitomises much of the life and history, maritime and ecclesiastical, of these regions. Lapp *mores* can be studied here without the discomfort of sharing their life. There is a surprising collection of ecclesiastical statuary from churches to the south and photographs of medieval monastic sites in the Lofoten islands.

Above all, Tromsø is the entrance to the extreme north. On leaving it, even by road, there is the sensation of adventure into the real Arctic.

# CHAPTER 11
# FINNMARK AND FINLAND

*Here the light of the setting sun lingers on till sunrise
bright enough to dim the light of the stars. . . . Only thus
far—and here rumour seems truth—does the world
extend.*

Tacitus, *Germania*

At Tromsø Norway swells from its giraffe-like neck into
a broad cranium. This is Finnmark. For the first time
since entering Nordland the motorist has a choice of
routes to the extreme north.

At a hamlet called Oteren, eighteen kilometres north
of the junction at Vollan, the road on the west side of
Lyngenfjord follows the coast up to Alta, nearly four
hundred and ninety kilometres from Tromsø; on the
east side of the same fjord, at Skibotn, twenty-eight
kilometres from its head, an alternative road follows a
salmon river, Skibotnelv, over the mountains into
Finland; then, at Palojoensuu, it turns north-east over
the border again into Norway, continuing through
Kautokeino to Alta.

At Oteren I took the road through Finland, leaving
the coastal route for my return journey. This northern
road was still able to surprise with its beauty, both along
the grey east bank of the fjord and up the course of
Skibotnelv: there was a wildness in the countryside
different from the more southern Arctic regions of
Norway. As it climbed to the untenanted Norwegian
frontier post, reindeer in small flocks of four to eight
moved among the stunted ash and birch, their pelts in
early June blending with the brown stubs of last year's
undergrowth. It was not yet the end of winter: icy gusts
came cuttingly off the snow-covered slopes and the river,
with restricted fishing rights in all its reaches, was now a

torrent too fast for the first salmon to make their way up.
At the summit there was a wilderness of snow, rock
and scrub, a no-man's-land between two nations. Here,
unsheltered from the winds, was the framework of a
Lapp tent, abandoned for the summer; and, in front of
it, a sledge, rough skis, decaying deer skins, firewood
piled up for the winter.

In the spring the Lapps move down to the coast,
leaving the mountain mosses to grow for winter
reindeer fodder. On this plateau none except a Lapp can
live: even the most primitive form of cultivation is
impossible in this barren, blasted, unchartered scrub-
land many metres above the line of mountain fir. Yet
in all three Scandinavian countries, and in Russia, it
is this kind of terrain they choose for their winter
settlements: its unrelieved desolation marks it out
unmistakenly as Lapland. Give a Lapp a milder climate
in winter and he will sneak back to his settlement in a
snow-field. He may make a comfortable fortune by
trading, come as far south as Trøndelag, and there (as
has happened), after building a house, live in a tent in
an isolated stretch of the neighbouring countryside.
Some, however, engage in trade and become sedentary.

There was no Norwegian frontier post, but the
Finnish station on this mountain plain was manned in a
military fashion reminiscent of pre-war Germany. At
this season perhaps three cars crossed in a day, but
passports, luggage, car papers, were all examined and
five shillings charged for a piece of paper which an official
gummed to the rear window of the car indicating its
country of origin. It was a humourless, bureaucratic
proceeding.

The road across the frontier followed the line of the
River Könkämä, which was also the border between
Finland and Sweden. There was an hotel on the shore
of lake Kilpisjärvi, about twenty kilometres beyond the
Finnish post, the only stopping place in a wild, rocky
expanse of inhospitable heath.

# Norway

What at first appeared an arbitrary boundary unquestionably divided two peoples and two cultures, for
the Finns have no Scandinavian characteristics: ethni-
cally they belong to another European family and their
language, one of the most difficult in Europe, has no
resemblance to the Nordic group: their commonest
words are unrecognisable. Even the behaviour of the
Finns is a world apart from their neighbours: they eat
raw fish, react violently to alcohol, sit silently in
company for hours, carry knives (it is said in Helsinki
that the Monday newspapers carry a list of persons
stabbed the previous week-end); but at the same time
they have taste in design, particularly in ceramics and
furnishings, and their architecture can be impressive
and functional. But from Helsinki to Lake Inari in
Finnish Lapland they live in isolation from Europe,
pursuing a way of life that has changed little from the
time they were occupied first by Sweden, then by
Russia.

Moreover, they venerate the sauna. It is a ritual, if
not a substitute for religion. They are said to build
their sauna hut before their home; and there comes a
point in every relationship with a Finnish family when
a friend joins the household in the sauna on a Saturday
afternoon. In the country it is something the guest
cannot escape, for there is no other means of washing.
If the visitor is wise he will avoid the accessories,
especially in winter, when, steamed to boiling point,
he is expected to plunge into a hole broken in the surface
of an ice-covered lake. Only in this way is he said to
benefit from the full reinvigoration the sauna offers.
Special wood is used for the benches to prevent the
scorching of backsides.

The Kilpisjärvi Tourist Hotel was sprucely Finnish in its comfort, food and furnishings. From the
dining-room it was possible to look out both into
Norway and Sweden, across a still-frozen lake. It was a
typical mountain hotel in an uninhabited wasteland.

# Finnmark and Finland

The first fifty miles south-east from Kilpisjärvi belonged exclusively to the Lapps, an unforested plateau, stretching into a wilderness in which a man can wander for days without a human encounter. At this season no Lapps were to be seen: there were no Finnish homesteads. Among the stumpy trees that might have been struck by lighting, and alongside snow-covered lakes, or in marshland, there were grouse, stray deer, wild duck for anyone's taking; there were these abandoned wooden frameworks of the Lapps' tents, sometimes isolated, sometimes in clusters or mingled with more solid wooden shacks. Always near by stood the fenced enclosures or corrals into which the reindeer are herded and sorted after migration. Usually the encampments were sited four or five hundred yards off the road: along the road itself, at intervals of a few miles, was a signpost, indicating the name of each place, and a shelter for goods delivered from more civilised regions.

At Palojoensuu there is a route north to Enonteckio, then west again towards another border point on the road connecting northern Finland with Alta. Wherever the road descended to the lower uplands, there was thick, tidy, carefully controlled afforestation. There was no trace of Lapp occupation: only when it climbed again above the level of cultivation, were the Lapp spoors scattered over the plateau.

There is a sameness in the Finnish countryside that quickly palls. Over the border again into Norway, the variety was unending. The goal for the day was Kautokeino, a Lapp town on the road to Alta. Like Karasjok, another Lapp town on a parallel road to the east over trackless mountains, Kautokeino was destroyed by the Germans in 1944 during the retreat from Finland. The site only is ancient. Apart from a handful of Norwegians, who run the school, the bank, general store and hostel, the whole population, perhaps 3,000, is Lapp.

# Norway

There was an eerie stillness about the place in the evening sunlight which, acting as a filter, gave sharper definition to the rugged countryside; then later, towards midnight, the colouring of the grass, trees, houses and rocks grew more mellow and intense. Men who have lived for years in these places never cease to be excited by the sight of the sea and land transformed by the rays of the sun striking from the north. By the degree of its brightness they learn to tell the exact hour of night. At the end of the old day it weakens; then (instead of a slow dawn) it waxes in power from the first minutes of the next day.

Only for the Lapps does the Norwegian Government run boarding schools. The school at Kautokeino is experimental and clean, with accommodation for two hundred Lapp boarders and some Norwegian day pupils. The sleeping quarters are cleaner and more spacious than in the average English public school: there is a carpenter's shop, art studio, cookery room,

*Lapp girls*

sports facilities. Lapp and Norwegian are mixed and there is distinction only in their dress: the Lapps wear their blue national costume, common to children and adults. It calls for a peculiar dedication on the part of the staff to work in the heart of Finnmark on the training of a younger generation of Lapps in a way of life in conflict with their parents': it is too early to judge their success. It was said to me that the intelligence of the Lapp pupils was on a level with the Norwegians: but they lacked motives for study. Their reindeer were somewhere in the mountains, and from time to time children returned surreptitiously at night to their nomadic families.

The origin of the Lapp people is an unsolved ethnical problem. The earliest and still tenable assumption is that they came from central Asia, an earlier migratory group than the Finns, and passed immediately to the Arctic uplands. In the early nineteenth century it was thought they were descendants of a primitive polar race, the prototype of the dwarf people of Norse mythology. Then a German ethnologist believed he had refuted this theory and placed their origin in the east in the last millennium B.C.; others set their migration further back in time: they were said to have followed the receding ice-cap with their reindeer. Finally it was asserted that they had always been where they now are.

All this was little more than guesswork or, at best, a working hypothesis for field study.

The first archaeological discoveries bearing on Lapp origins were made in this century by a Norwegian, Anders Nummerdal.

On Komsafjell, overhanging the northern end of Alta, Nummerdal found some implements, including primitive skis, dating from 8000 B.C., and deduced that these regions of Lapland[1] were inhabited throughout the Ice Age by a people he called pro-Lapps, who existed as the Eskimoes do today on the ice-covered coastal strip of Greenland. There the question remains.

---

[1] Lapland, as a geographical designation, is strictly a province of Sweden. Here it is taken as the area inhabited by Lapps.

# Norway

The Lapps were the only race in Europe not to be touched by Christianity in the Middle Ages. In the late sixteenth century missionaries from the south converted them from a primitive animism to orthodox Lutheranism: then, before the new religion had taken roots, a Swedish missionary, Lestadius, preached among them an extreme form of hell-fire revivalism, which resulted in atrocities, violence and sometimes murder. Today the Lapp religion is known as Lestardianism: in Kautokeino and Karasjok, and in the hills between Alta and Skaidi, they have their own churches. But still in certain places there are relics of their old altars known as oracle stones: the most revered of them stands at the entrance to Laksefjord. Occasionally, on these stones, jugs of milk and honey are found left as offerings as in the days of their old gods.

The earliest Lapp idols were usually rocks of fantastic shapes or curiously formed tree stumps, sometimes treated sculpturally. Ordinarily the sacrifice was a reindeer, in exceptional cases a horse: other objects, such as coins and ornaments, were sometimes thrown into the sacrifice.

When witchcraft revived in Norway in the seventeenth century, the Lapps were believed to be expert sorcerers. It was rumoured that the great Swedish victories of that century were due to Lapp conjurers which the Swedish generals kept in their trains. For instance, John Rous, the English diarist, has this entry after Gustavus Adolphus's victory at Breitenfeld in September 1631: 'A Jesuit at Strasbourg, after the Swedish victory, made his prayer to this effect: "Lords and ladies, let us pray to God . . . to defend us against the devil of Sweden and all his helps—the conjurers and witches of Lapland, by whose enchantments these Swedish devils fly about among us."'

It was to disprove this charge that the first scientific survey of Lapland was made by a Swede in 1648. The result was that the Lapps emerged from fable into history.

# Finnmark and Finland

The road to the north-west from Kautokeino passed over the mountains to the head waters of the Altaelv, then down a gorge to the plateau where the torrent fell into the fjord. Between here and Kirkenes lies the paradise of fishermen. The rights on these mountain streams sell at exorbitant prices to wealthy Americans, who travel up to the main centres on small seaplanes from Tromsø. However, on 7 June the salmon were not yet moving up the rivers, though fishermen were trawling for them in the open fjord at Alta and Hammerfest: in the early morning they pulled into the quay, displayed their glistening catch on deck, and settled for a price with the hotel proprietors. There is good fishing in the fjords: anyone, for twenty-five shillings, can take out a year's licence at the post office. It entitles him to fish 'anywhere', which means in any unrestricted place.

At Alta it was almost another three hundred kilometres to Kirkenes. There were reports that Lapps were out on the mountains north of the town with their herds: they have been called the 'people of eight seasons' and it is difficult in summer-time to get precise information of their whereabouts.[1] Then they seem to settle nowhere for more than a few weeks.

The road out of Alta climbed quickly into the mountains. After twenty kilometres, standing a few yards back from the road, was a Lapp, with two dogs at his feet, outside a rough shack. He asked for a cigarette and took the entire packet. Then he explained that he formed part of the advance party of Lapps from Kautokeino, migrating to the coast with its herds: the main body was still in the hills to the east and was expected tomorrow. His hut in the snow was their assembly point.

Inside there were two more dogs, much gentler than the Norwegian farm dogs, originally crossbred with the

---

[1] The eight seasons distinguished by the Lapps are early spring, spring, early summer, summer, late summer, autumn, late autumn and winter.

wolf. The Lapp's son and two grandsons squatted in a corner watching the red reindeer meat stewing in a pan on an open chimney-less fire; the floor was covered with skins. He enunciated Norwegian clearly. A bottle-opener hung from his ornamental belt: he asked whether I had any schnaps.

Where was his wife? He pointed higher up the road: she was watching the herds. There she was, sitting on a rock, and around her, on all sides, the herds, perhaps two or three hundred deer of different breeds, wandering antler to stern, compact like a flock of sheep, half-wild, callow, frightened creatures that only these men had learnt to control like domestic beasts. To the un-initiated they were all reindeer, but the Lapp had a dozen distinct terms for them according to the sex, shape, age of each, the formation of its antlers, its cry, colour of hair and behaviour. In the same way, he had a name for every feature in the countryside, for the smallest meadow, brook, marsh or slope.

*Lapps on their way to a wedding*

The deer appeared half-famished after the winter. As they crossed the road, they stopped to lick the salt that had been scattered on it to break up the ice. In summer they graze on herbs, grasses and shrubs, in the autumn on fungi, and in winter on lichen. They nibble at a leaf or shoot, then move on. As they passed they made a curious crackling noise. I learnt later that it came not from their hooves, but from a tendon in the toes which at each step is stretched across a small bone. In the night this clinking sound keeps the herd together. There is an elaborate system of allocating herding rights, worked out and imposed by inspectors, who sometimes use aeroplanes to enforce them.

A short distance beyond the place where the Lapp lady sat there was a church, set five hundred yards to the right of the road in a trackless and isolated plateau. Here the Lapps worshipped and celebrated their weddings when they were in this district.

The Lapps have a word, *sita*, which is used for families that join together to tend their reindeer in a common herd in a common grazing area. The ownership of the animals is private, but the tending of the herd collective. Each owner has his own registered mark—a private pattern of nicks cut in the animal's ear. The practice is immemorial and the combination limitless.

It is possible to travel for weeks in Finnmark and not meet a herd: on my way south across this plateau there was not a single stray animal to be seen. They had moved over to the islands.

These herds are the travelling fortune of the Lapps and their means of livelihood. They eat their meat, supplemented by fish in summer; they drink their milk and produce from it a pungent cheese; the antlers are sold to tourists for decoration; the skins are used for footwear, caps, jackets and carpeting, the bones for handles of knives. In winter the reindeer provide the fast means of transport across the snows.

The Lapp is always friendly. He has a culture and is proud of it. While he is ready to take benefits from the Norwegian Government, he remains a member of an independent race: not even the Russians can check their migrations from one country to another.

Almost indistinguishable now from the non-Lapp population of Finnmark are the Quains. They belong to a race that may have settled here even earlier than the Lapps. They are stocky, large-headed, olive-tinted people, with tartar features; they are related to the Finns, possess fixed homes, live mostly by fishing and have their own language, Quensk.

At Skaidi, eighty-nine kilometres from Alta, the road forked: to the west it followed the south side of Repparfjord to the ferry across to Kvaløy, on which Hammerfest is situated, to the east it trailed along the banks of the Arctic fjords and cut across the mountains between them for three hundred and seventy-five kilometres to the Russian border at Kirkenes.

This is the most northerly highway of Europe. It confronts the Arctic and no land lies north of it except Bear Island and Spitzbergen. The fjords have an atmosphere different again from the north-western fjords of the same province. They are tidal. The roads over the dividing mountains are closed for the greater part of the year and a sense of isolation hangs over the countryside. The waters are greyer, the strips of cultivation more rare, the light changes quickly. Life along the shores depends almost entirely on fish. Whole tracts of the hinterland are treeless and the road is worse than any in Europe; stopping-places lie sometimes sixty kilometres apart.

Lakselv is the unofficial capital of this region and it offers moderate comfort for salmon fishers. It lies at the head of the deepest of the north Arctic fjords; but beyond is a scrubby waste. At this time of the year the climate changed with the altitude of the road: at fjord level it was summer, but over the mountain beyond Isfjord, the road passed between walls of hard-packed snow ten feet high—a man stood fishing through a hole pierced in the centre of a frozen lake. Tarmfjord, from the hill above, seemed to belong to the world of the south: blue waters and warm sun on the subdued shades of the fishermen's homes; near Gandvik, in sunshine, the Arctic road was like a deserted stretch of the French Corniche. At Tana there was an Orthodox church, a reminder that the country over the border belonged to Finland until the peace treaty in 1944. June was hardly summer: a month later there were buses along this road, based on Rovaniemi, just south of the Arctic Circle in Finland. Travel agencies there organised regular all-in price tours to Finnmark that included calls at Kirkenes, Hammerfest and Lapp towns (presumably Kautokeino or Karasjok), with accommodation in first-class hotels. The season had not opened.

Kirkenes stands less than an hour's walk from the Russian border. In all hotels and public places hung notices in Norwegian warning the visitor against trespassing in the frontier area: no one should fish, drive, photograph or ramble too near the border. These were safeguards to protect Norwegian citizens against Russian retaliation.

The road to the nearest border check ended abruptly at a small farm sloping down to a narrow strip of water. On the Norwegian side there was an untenanted guardpost and, behind it, on a spur of land, a look-out, also deserted. Ahead I counted five barriers: a pole four feet above the road surface, a barbed-wire mesh, a ditch, a fencing, then, scarcely visible in the sunlight, a trip wire. No Norwegian flag flew from the mastpole. A sharp twist in the road concealed the Russian checkpoint. In the fifteen minutes I stood there no man, animal or object appeared. Beyond there was fir forest, planted tightly in the Finnish manner: this was formerly Finland and seized by the Russians in 1944.

Last year the border had been opened and restricted entrance into Russia allowed, mainly for the purchase of vodka at the nearest Russian store. Later this year, in August, the Russians raised their barrier, but the Norwegians kept theirs down: they had problems enough controlling alcoholism on their side.

# Norway

Here, as in the Karelian isthmus and in the central portion of Finland and other stolen territories, the native population had fled before the Russians. In their place Stalin had planted families that had suffered losses in the fighting in each of the annexed areas. He was determined never to have the problem of an ethnic minority demanding reunion with its mother nation.

For forty kilometres I drove south along the frontier road. There was an occasional military truck, a lonely rowing-boat moored to a pier, but no trace of a defence position. Cultivation came down to the fringe of the small frontier lakes and on the far side there was again thick afforestation. A radio mast was planted on the highest of a line of hills, and it was possible to pick out the chimney stacks of Tollevi, which the Russians were converting into an industrial centre.

In my short two days at Kirkenes the birch trees suddenly budded. The growth was almost visible: it starts late, about mid-June, but is continuous day and night. Vegetables here are said to be the finest in the world; once the seeds sprout there is no darkness to stop their growth.

Kirkenes was the ultimate port of call for the steamers from Bergen. There was one due on Friday, 10 June, which would put in at Hammerfest the following afternoon: the sea route was the only alternative to the haul back along the rough north Arctic highway. But before I could fix a passage a cargo-boat steamed into the fjord: it could be sailing only west. The captain agreed to load my car on deck and give me a cabin: he expected to sail sometime after midnight.

Norwegian sailors, unlike British, can return drunk from absence ashore, then instantly set about preparations for sailing as though they had not touched alcohol for a fortnight. This they did: and the *Vardø*, built at Moss in 1953, steamed out at about two-thirty in the morning into Varangerfjord, passing the fortress town of Vadsø on her port side.

# Finnmark and Finland

It was from Vadsø near here that Nansen and Hjalmar Johnsen set out in the *Fram*, now enshrined in a museum in Oslo, on 21 July 1893. Their intention was to reach the North Pole. After following the Siberian coast, they turned north until the *Fram*, on Christmas Day the same year, got stuck in pack-ice and drifted northwards. In the spring the two explorers left their ship and pushed towards the Pole on sledges. But they abandoned their attempt to reach it and turned south to Franz Joseph Island, drifting most of the way on ice in the company of polar bears. They passed a dark Arctic winter in a stone igloo, living on seal meat and broth, using walrus blubber for their lamps.

At the end of their hibernation they were picked up by a clean-shaven Englishman, wearing checked tweeds and smelling of perfumed soap. This was Frederick Jackson, from the British yacht *Windward*, who had been left with a companion on the ice for research work. They reached Vadsø on 13 August 1896 and received the welcome of heroes. At Hammerfest they were greeted by Sir George Baden-Powell, who had sailed from England in search of them.

From four to five miles out to sea this north Arctic coast looked inhospitable, almost uninhabitable. An occasional tanker, bound presumably for Murmansk, passed on the starboard side, without an exchange of signals; Russian trawlers of modern design were busy further to the north. Beyond, to the north-west, lay the group of islands forming Spitzbergen. This was near the top of the globe: the difficulty of reaching any but local stations on the radio was a reminder that the earth curved more sharply at its summit, thus increasing the distance between the wireless waves.

Honningsvåg was tucked at the foot of a conical, treeless and precipitous rock on the southern and sheltered side of the island on which stood the North Cape. It was the only port of call before Hammerfest. Like other towns in Finnmark it had been totally rebuilt

since the war under the initiative of a special department in Oslo, which, for distance, might have been
supervising the construction of a new town in Constan-
tinople or Morocco. Behind the port, five rows of fences
on the hill-side protected it from avalanches. There was
rain, grey sky and a silver sea on this mid-June afternoon.

These waters first became known in England
through Chancellor's voyage in 1553. After a storm off
the north-west coast had separated his ship from
Willoughby's, he passed the north tip of Norway,
which he called the North Cape, and sailed east in the
direction of Kirkenes. Eventually he reached the mouth
of the Dvina river in north Russia, then travelled overland to the Czar in Moscow. He did not discover a
new route to India, but he came back with trading
privileges for English merchants. He was hailed as the
discoverer of a new passage to Russia: in fact it was
known to the Vikings in the days of King Alfred.

The *Vardø* did not round the North Cape, but sailed
beneath it through a narrow channel across which, in
August, the Lapps swim their reindeer to feed on the
summer mosses there.

# CHAPTER 12
# HAMMERFEST AND SOUTH

*What was Njal doing? asked Hallgard.*
*He was busy sitting still, they replied.*

Njal's Saga

Hammerfest may not be the end of the world, but there is no more northerly town anywhere: Honningsvåg is reckoned a village, Kirkenes lies on a lower latitude, Juno in Alaska on the same as Oslo.
Viewed from the sea it looks attractive, but there is nothing to keep a visitor here. On Saturday evenings there is a dance in the Grand Hotel and the cinema changes its film every day, but the only old building to survive the war is the wooden mortuary chapel in the cemetery. A rocky hill comes steeply down to the shore, leaving only a small strip on which the town is built.

The inhabitants live by fishing: in mid-June, as in Alta, they were trawling in the fjord for salmon on their course to the mountain streams; a large deep-freezing plant, the Findus industry, accounted for the same penetrating odour of fish as at Stamsund. In *Njal's Saga* Njal is described as 'busy sitting still': this appeared the main preoccupation of the people of Hammerfest. When the temperature dropped, they ambled arm in arm down the main street.

In winter, presumably, they slept; but when the *Vardø* tied up in the early hours of this Sunday morning the whole town was active: there were more people about, more cars, there was more talk, more sitting than on the following or on any other morning.

There are two buildings of restricted interest: the Lutheran church, on a rise to the south of the town, constructed on the pattern of the racks on which the fishermen here and in Lofoten set out their catch of cod to dry in the Arctic winds, and the Catholic church, overlooking the port and the seemingly endless fjord. It is a more inspired building, the successor of the wooden Gothic structure erected a hundred years

*Lapp followed by his reindeer sleigh*

ago by the first Prefect Apostolic of the North Pole. There is also a hospital run by nuns. On the ground floor there are baths used by the local fishermen, principally on Saturdays.

This was the end of my journey. Since leaving Oslo, even with two short hops by steamer, I had travelled 3,443 kilometres on the worst roads in Europe at the worst time of the year. During the eight days I was to stay here, there was little to do but read: soon even the stimulus to read faded. I tried more Ibsen, but his world of the south seemed a foreign country in Hammerfest, which was orientated to whales and the Arctic ice-cap. An old French book entitled *Norvège*, by H. Le Roux, published in 1895, contained some interesting chapters. 'La femme et l'amour' was the longest in the book; there was another, 'La vie morale'. By chance, in the middle of my reading, a French destroyer called on a goodwill visit. For two days the girls stopped sitting; each found her *matelot*. A Norwegian friend once remarked that I must forgive her compatriots much because of the climate they endured. It was clear that in places like this there was little else but love-making to engage the people.

This was the pursuit also of the first tourist of distinction to these parts, Louis Philippe, later king of the French. In fear of assassination after his father, Philippe Égalité, had been guillotined, he fled to Norway. At Bodø he stayed with the Lutheran pastor, then crossed to the Lofotens. Houses, rooms, even beds associated with him are shown to the tourist today. From Hammerfest he visited the North Cape: he was disguised as a trader and spent the night below the Cape in a fisherman's hut.

From Alta he crossed Finnmark into Sweden. At Muoniska he was entertained by a Swedish pastor, Kolstrøm, and in return seduced his sister-in-law: the son of the liaison migrated to Norway and settled in the district of the river Tana, where there is diluted Bourbon blood to this day.

The most attractive characteristic of this least attractive of French kings was his grateful recollection of Norwegian hospitality. When the Norwegian painter, Peder Balke, held an exhibition in Paris, Louis Philippe patronised it and commissioned for Versailles seventy paintings, including a portrait of himself and his travelling companion standing against the barren rock of the North Cape. Louis Philippe lost his throne before the commission was executed.

There were no walks on the rocky surroundings of Hammerfest: acres only of treeless rock. In winter, storms, ice and blizzards make for poor skiing conditions. A Catholic priest here must be, compulsorily, a saint, scholar or solitary or a combination of the three. If anywhere in the world a case could be presented for the marriage of the Catholic clergy, it is at Hammerfest: the conditions of a priest's life here are unlikely to recur elsewhere. In the evening the clouds, squatting all day on the rock that dominates the town, swirl down to roof-top level and shut off all visibility. The sense of isolation can become unendurable: a single man in his prime, posted here by order, not by request, needs a special providence to maintain his mental balance.

At Hammerfest I plotted my return. From Oteren, about ninety kilometres from Tromsø, I had taken the inland route north through Finland to Alta; on my return (as I had intended) I followed the long coastal road back to Oteren. From Oteren to Narvik I was forced to retrace my tracks, but from Narvik south to Bodø, and from Bodø over Saltfjell to Mo i Rana and Mosjøen it was again country I had not seen.

Altafjord, with its cold, blue, sharp-peaked mountains peering out from heavy clouds, was grand even in the slanting rain: a vast, sombre, at times sullen stretch of unending water. For weeks the Viking fleets would lie concealed in its deep inlets. In the last war it was the hide-out of the German battleship *Tirpitz*. Discovered and torpedoed by one-man submarines, she crept south to Tromsø and with 12,000 men on board was sunk there by bombs on 12 November 1944. There were parts of the fjord very thinly peopled; large, occasional stretches of pasture shared among two or three homesteads; perilous, zigzag climbs between mountains, then a quick descent to sea level.

At the summit of Kvaehangfjell, on the first day out from Alta, a Lapp family had pitched its tent. The framework of stakes was covered with canvas and turf; outside, on a single pole, stood a store-case for reindeer meat, and a sledge, built like a boat with stern, keel, bulwarks and ribs, the stern and keel plank forming a runner.

Smoke rose from a cavity in the centre of the tent. Three unwashed dogs roamed outside and a blizzard swept the loose earth into a dusty cloud in front of the slit opening. An old Lapp lady wrapped in skins was huddled over an open fire with three small children snuggling by her; the air was thick and it was difficult at first to make out all the objects. Later I noticed that the old lady was stitching shoes. She offered me a pair; there were also hats, gloves and belts at her feet, but what surprised me most was the extent of floor area, with distinct sections apportioned to sleeping, working and cooking, the unjoined wooden planks laid over the wet earth covered with skins. There was a board for *tablo*, a Lapp game not unlike 'fox and geese'. In a corner was a cot in which small children were carried over the snow in winter.

*Lapp infant in cot*

Lapps thrive in this squalor. Less than a hundred years ago it is said that when old Lapp folk became too infirm to trek over the mountains with their families, they were left behind to die unattended in these tents. The corpse froze and was buried on the family's return. Some writers believe that the Lapps used another method of disembarrassing themselves of their old people: strapped to a sleigh alive, they were shot down the steep snow-covered precipice into the fjord. This is the end they expected and they submitted to it un-complainingly. It is thought also that when an old woman was near death she would be given a cold bath to hasten her dying.

Outside, the mountain summit fell sharply into another inlet of Altafjord, and I wondered whether the old lady caring for these three grandchildren, was not expecting her end to be hastened.

Until Narvik was reached there were still few cars. The majority of tourists setting out for Finnmark were forced to return hundreds of kilometres from their goal. In their planning no account had been taken of the bad roads or the delays for ferries. It can be reckoned a good day's driving in northern Norway if two hundred kilometres are covered. At Narvik, Bodø and Mo i Rana, many miles to the south, disillusioned motorists had turned back or attempted to ship their cars south. Garages were crammed with battered Volkswagens.

Possibly also the mosquitoes of the far north deterred them. Guide books cannot leave the subject aside. These mosquitoes, in fact, are a species found only here: they are large and persistent, with a fierce bite that can cause long sickness, but it is only in the brief peak of high summer that they tease and bite: moreover, they can always be seen and slaughtered. Nineteenth-century travel writers discuss methods of combating them, usually in an appendix. One academic tourist invented his own flea-proof and dirt-proof nightshirt. 'It is constructed of calico', he explained, 'in the usual manner, but made long enough to tie over the feet and hands; and thus none but the very industrious fleas, who may discover the secret passage by the neck, can penetrate to the skin. ... A pony could carry one of these luxurious garments with the rest of the luggage.'

Midsummer night in Norway is celebrated with bonfires all over the country: they are lit on every valley farm and *seter* and skerry on which there is any habitation. The custom dates from pagan times but it is still meaningful in a country where winter and summer are such disparate seasons.

This midsummer night I stayed with Magnus Pettersen at Ballangen, on the south side of Narvik fjord. There was no darkness or even twilight, but in the evening rain the further bank of the shallow inlet became suddenly a line of bonfires. It was like a last salute to an old year. From now the days would begin to close in to a long winter.

Pettersen was the headmaster of the school in Ballangen, and proud of his position and school: it was new and the State had spared no expense in equipping it. He was proud also that his family had lived in this valley since the thirteenth century, peasants in origin but cultured for centuries before the French and English farmer had any education.

The preferential treatment given by law to the family of the late owner of a farm, when it comes on to the market, explains the stability of peasant inhabitants of these valleys. Provided a man can prove the title of his family, he can re-purchase the estate that once belonged to his ancestors: if he has not the ready cash, then he can keep his claim alive by declaring it at the sessions every ten years. This is called 'Odel's right'. When the claimant or *odelsman* has raised the money, he can evict the occupier. For protection against such claimants all Norwegian freeholders keep a strict record of their pedigree.

The purpose of the law was to entice emigrants back to Norway and also to prevent advantage being taken of a farmer in a bad year. Certainly it fixes the affections of the peasant on his native place; on the other hand, it makes it difficult for an outsider to enter the community, if his right to a newly acquired farm might have to be surrendered to a relative of the man from whom he has bought it. Pettersen, the headmaster of Ballangen school, knew his pedigree.

There is an efficiency and lack of fuss in Norwegian schools thanks to a long tradition of universal education.

For the past hundred and fifty years every child in Norway has been taught to read and write. Valleys, in which there was no church or road, had their schoolmaster. Where a valley stretched too far for one school, it was portioned out into districts and the teacher devoted a number of weeks to each in succession; where there was no school-house, instruction was carried out on the farm. The cost was met by the community: every man paid the same small sum, whether he had one child or six. In addition, all the peasants were taught a little history and science: the old schoolbooks were admirable. Knowledge tests before confirmation provided an examination system on a national scale. Still today remote districts have their itinerant schoolmaster or *omgangsskollaerer*, who goes from place to place with blackboard and books on his back. Any person who does not receive the statutory seven years' schooling can sue the local authorities for neglect.

Today, as in the past, confirmation is taken as the initiation ceremony into full membership of the Lutheran Church. All but a fraction of the people go through the ceremony, and for this fraction a civil confirmation, conducted by the Mayor in the city hall of Oslo, forms a substitute. It is the equivalent in Scandinavia of the twenty-first birthday celebration in England. Substantial presents in kind and cash are expected from all relatives. Once confirmed in the Church, a Lutheran changing or abandoning his religion has formally to opt out: he visits his pastor who gives him a signed statement that he is no longer a Church member. The pastor may consider it his duty to dissuade the applicant. However, most non-believers do not take the trouble of going through this formality: atheist, heretic and heresiarch still keep their nominal membership of the Church.

In a country where individual Catholics are separated sometimes by hundreds of miles, a traveller is loaded with messages on his way from one Catholic homestead to another. In England greetings from person to person are conveyed negligently, but not in Norway. As I left the Pettersens I was given messages to deliver over many miles on the road south.

# Hammerfest and South

At Fauske there is a small railroad towards the Swedish border up a steep mountain pass to Furulund, where iron ore is mined. It was off the tourist route, remote even at the height of the season. The train, with a miscellany of trucks for cars, iron ore, passengers and general goods, crawled through a series of a dozen tunnels in the space of an hour to a height of 5,000 feet; at the exit of every tunnel the mountain stream broadened into a lake. There were some small farmsteads with a few cows; at Sulitjelma there was a hotel, but no fish: at this altitude the river was polluted by ore. It was another extremity of this Arctic world.

On the Sunday there was a confirmation in the church that served the people of Furulund. It was more like a local holiday than an ecclesiastical event. Celebrations were communal: a banquet was prepared at the hotel for the participants and their families, and flags flew from every mast in the valley.

Above Furulund was Jakobsbakken, another eight miles up the mountain road and another thousand feet. There was nothing here but a settlement of miners: not even a café or place to rest, for no tourist visited it. Snow still lay on the plateau in these last days of June. Copper dust coloured the streams and swamps and wild deer moved in the scrub; there were red and mauve mosses beside the mountain road, with wild flowers growing everywhere, so thickly in places that for these few summer weeks it was like walking through a wild rock garden among the snow.

Places like this remove all sense of time: there is no urgency to move on, though there may be little to retain you. Hundreds of miles from Hammerfest the district was still within the Arctic Circle. No one had written about it. Only the executive engaged in the mining business came here. Even the hotel was not sited for tourists.

It was a world untouched by history. There was no reason for coming or for going. Everything stood still.

# Norway

In 1870 a Scottish traveller in Norway complained there was nothing to see in the towns or villages. What was old has been burned at one time or another. Royal residences outside Oslo are constructed in timber; national archives, stored in timber buildings, have been lost in fires. The interest of places can be discovered only by sharing the life of the people and listening to their talk. There is history in Norway but not in written records. There survive the occasional letter, the report, the account of the traveller. The rest of history is legend and local recollection.

# CHAPTER 13
## BODØ-MO i RANA-STEINKJER-WEST TRØNDELAG

*The devil in his old age becomes a monk.*

Norwegian Proverb

Bodø, at the tip of a long peninsula, is the most southerly town of any size in the Arctic Circle. In 1962 it became the terminus of the railway from Oslo, 1,316 kilometres or thirty-six hours by train to the south.

Founded in the nineteenth century, Bodø failed as a trading post, then prospered for twenty years from 1864 on shoals of herring, later still on the export of iron ore from Sulitjelma. Today it is a tourist centre, an important market town and a pivotal airbase in the NATO defence system. It has a fine coastline, particularly to the north: the summit of the Rønvik mountain outside the town is said to give the finest sight of the midnight sun, framed there between twin peaks among the island approaches. Twenty-four hour return flights from Oslo bring thousands of tourists to this viewpoint every summer. There is not an old building in the town, which was razed to the ground during the war, but today it has all the signs of expansion. The Gulf Stream gives it an ice-free harbour and a milder winter temperature than Oslo's. At Saltstraumen, twenty miles away, the sea pours through a narrow strait creating the most powerful maelstrom in the world; at Bodin, on the outskirts, is one of the few medieval churches of the north.

The airport above the fjord is very conscious of its Arctic position. A signpost there gives the startling information that it is shorter by an hour and forty-five minutes to fly to the North Pole than to Paris; but it is

more surprising to find within a five minutes' walk of
this signpost a settlement of English Dominican nuns
from their mother house at Stone, Staffordshire. For
ten days in early July I was the guest of this small
community of five Sisters.

There is something in the spirit of this Order that
makes it particularly suited to Norway: a readiness to
understand the mentality of a different people and to
enter into it without losing its own. Its success is there
to be seen, not merely in the kindergarten, the youth
club and hostel it runs, but in the way it has been
adopted by the town. In the streets old women and
infants greet the nuns; youths, now in jobs, once their
charges, talk to them on the station without any self-
consciousness. Their convent is an open house, night
and day: friends and strangers come for advice, holiday-
makers from the south looking for a bed, business
people and their families overdue for a friendly visit.
Their gaiety is a tonic to the district. Thanks to them
there is not a trace of anti-Catholic prejudice for miles
around.

It was at their suggestion that I crossed Skjerstadfjord
at Vågan to Skjerstad. It is a remote and lovely area: on
the mountains are herds of Norwegian goats, reared for
the compressed, brown, highly scented cheese that is an
acquired taste for the foreign palate. It has the colour
of khaki and the shape of a brick. In Norwegian homes
it is as inescapable as *lapskaus*. There is also *gammelost*,
or old cheese, reminiscent of Stilton in the last stages
of decay. Sugar and certain herbs are used in manufacturing it. When fresh, it is uneatable, but after many
years' keeping it decomposes, becomes powdery,
forming a sort of condiment rather than food. In its
perfect condition it is neither mouldy nor moist and
has a rich anchovy-paste flavour with a hint of par-
mesan.

The people of Bodø do not eat mackerel: they send it
all south, for there is an old belief that this fish is

carnivorous. This old prejudice was noted by Arch-deacon Coxe during his Norwegian journey in the eighteenth century: 'Mackerel [he wrote] might also be taken in much larger quantities, if many Norwegians were not prejudiced against eating them, from a strange notion that shoals of mackerel often attack and devour the human species when bathing at sea.' So Bodø exports its mackerel to Oslo where, when smoked, it becomes a delicacy all can afford. Nowhere in Norway are rabbits eaten: they are considered too closely allied to cats.

At Skjerstad church a serious wedding party was gathering. The church is impressively set on a hill overhanging the quay: its site is old, though nothing remains of the medieval building it replaced. In the cemetery lie three gravestones, the oldest in Norway, dating from the twelfth century.

From Bodø north to Hammerfest and south to Trondheim the sea remains the main means of travel. On this account the hamlets along the fjord have existed from ancient times in the same localities: roads are so few and usually impassable in winter that the map of these places has remained unaltered for centuries. In Finland the contrary holds. Until a hundred years ago people travelled always by lake. When roads were built new posting stations grew up at intervals in the forests: eventually many of the lakeside villages disappeared without trace, and the population was redistributed. Forestry replaced fish in the economy of the country.

It is a national custom of Norwegians to hang carpets on the walls of their living-rooms, but only in the newly-built cathedral at Bodø have I seen them used in this way as an ecclesiastical decoration: the Christian symbolism in the pattern is faint and elusive. Here as everywhere in Norway the pendant lights are poorly designed. While Norwegian furniture, at its best, is as attractive as in other Scandinavian countries, standard lights and shades ordinarily show a poor taste.

Only international trade agreements can explain the odd fact that most modern Norwegian furniture, ecclesiastical and domestic, is made in teak imported from Malaya. Presumably the ships transporting the dried fish from Bodø to Singapore return loaded with east-Asian timber. For similar reasons the streets of Santiago and other Chilean coastal towns are paved with stone from the Norwegian fjells, carried as ballast by ships that return to Norway with a cargo of meat.

The flowers of northern Norway, and more especially the blossom, make the visitor conscious of the late arrival of summer. On 5 July the laburnum was in full bloom. It was springtime here long after midsummer day. The midnight sun is last seen at Bodø on 10 July but the skies are more resplendent after its departure, when it sits a little further below the horizon. In Finland, at the same latitude, in August, the whole sky at midnight becomes an indescribable revelry of crimson, scarlet and vermilion: the glory of it is never forgotten. I have seen such skies against the waters of Lake Inari: it is the same at Bodø and all the way to the furthest north.

Lønsdal near the summit of Saltfjell is no more than a railway halt. There is nothing here but a comfortable hotel, staffed in summer by university students from small towns across the mountains in northern Sweden, but it is an excellent stopping place, particularly for fishermen: a stream a few yards away falls through a gorge into Rognan at the head of Skjerstadfjord along which Fauske and Bodø lie.

The more rugged section of Saltfjell begins a few miles south of Lønsdal, where the road climbs into a wasteland which is the true dividing area between north and south. This mountain plateau belongs to deer and any beasts that can survive on it; there are no habitations for men: not even Lapps use it. In the summer small white mountain flowers grow in crevices of the rock.

Across the summit, twenty-three miles south of

# Mo i Rana

Lønsdal, runs the line of the Arctic Circle. From June to August a café here is open for the benefit of tourists and also a post office with the polar circle postmark. In winter the road is impassable for five or six months; but at all times the train manages to cross Saltfjell through long tunnels of fencing covered with massive snow drifts: the train may be three or more hours late, but it arrives. A long winter train journey from Oslo to Bodø has the same kind of fascination and generates the same companionship as the old Orient Express.

The road descends from the summit through Dunderlandsdalen, following the river Rana to Mo i Rana at the head of Ranafjord. Mo i Rana itself has the atmosphere of neither the north nor south; it is a nondescript town brought into existence by the enterprise of the Meyer family, who purchased the place in 1860 and converted it from a trading station with Sweden, twenty-five miles away, into a modern industrial town. Today it is a centre of the Norwegian steel and iron industry. The main hotel, Meyergården, is the old residence of the Meyer family: its painted friezes and ceilings and spacious living-rooms are typical of the grand houses or *gårds* in which rich merchants lived a hundred years ago.

Boat-building is another industry initiated by the first Meyer, who found a market for over a thousand boats made from the fir trees of the Rana district; coffin making was a subsidiary. There are plans now to make Mo the Sheffield of Norway.

The one hundred and twenty kilometres between Mo and Mosjøen is probably the worst stretch of the north–south Norwegian highway: rutted and corrugated, it throws the cars from side to side of the earth surface so that a driver taking a corner rashly or braking suddenly ends up astride the road or in the fjord. At Mo there was a beautiful pass through high mountains down to Lake Øveruman in Sweden, re-entering Norway about forty kilometres south of Mosjøen, but I was told that it was in

165

fearful condition and decided to continue on the main road south.

The feeling of the Nordland countryside is caught best in the writings of Petter Dass, the most celebrated name in seventeenth-century Norwegian literature. Curiously he was the son of a Scot, Dundas, who had fled to Bergen from religious persecution in the time of Charles I. He was the pastor and poet of this province. The simple country people believed he controlled the powers of evil, that he wrestled with the devil and always won. His poetry gives a vivid picture of the people of Nordland, the conditions of their life and their ceaseless struggle with the sea: he writes of storms and shipwrecked fishermen holding desperately to the bottom of their upturned boats. The forces of nature always dominate, destroying one generation after another. For the instruction of the peasants he composed several collections of religious songs and a rhymed version of Luther's Catechism. From 1689 Dass (the Norwegian form his father chose for the family name) was pastor of Alstahaug, an attractive church with an onion spire on the same island as Sandnessjøen, where on my journey north I had caught the coastal steamer for the Lofoten islands.

From Mosjøen to Grong there was no alternative to the main road I had followed three months earlier. By mid-July the scene was different: snow had melted in all the high places of the road, there was a luxuriance of mountain ash and birch in full leaf and the wind blew warm from the south west. Norwegians on holiday were beginning to pluck the *moltebaer*, an orange berry shaped like a raspberry, that grows only in Norway and is rightly considered a luxury. Found mainly on high marshland, its leaf is shaped like a geranium's: the flower, white with a yellow centre, is seldom more than six inches above the ground. It tastes best when freshly picked, but at all times it can be bought, canned or bottled, in the larger towns.

# Steinkjer

Steinkjer in North Trøndelag, at the head of the Trondheim fjord, is a newly-rebuilt, not unattractive timber trading town at which the road forks to the east and west sides of the fjord. The new church by the bridge contains work by Jakob Weidemann, one of the finest living Norwegian painters. On Sunday 17 July there was no service there: the pastor was ministering in the country to the west, at Egge, where his people had followed him in a cavalcade of cars.

*Moltebaer*

The Lutheran Sunday service retains the framework of the Catholic Mass: in fact, its slow divergence from the old ritual partly explains why the Norwegian peasants of the sixteenth century were unaware that the Reformation had overtaken them. Later more lessons were introduced and an increasing number of hymns. The *Credo* remained in the old form, except for the substitution of *alminnelig* (ordinary) for *Catholic* in the definition of the Church.

After the offertory song the Lutheran pastor, clothed up to now in alb and ruff, retired behind the altar and reappeared in a black robe. The sermon followed. It showed no appreciation of the daily lot of the people, the text being illuminated by other texts, one parable by another; yet the handsome, white-haired, ruddy-faced, late middle-aged pastor was manifestly sincere: what he said might have been taken without alteration of a word from a seventeenth-century book of homilies. Evangelicism, pure and unadulterated, is insufficient to hold the active allegiance of the average Norwegian to the Church of his baptism. I recalled the comment of an Oslo friend who walked out of Trinity Church in Akersgate after a sermon in which the preacher, interpreting the gospel literally, exhorted his scant congregation to sell all they had and give to the poor. She regarded this as incompatible with her parental obligations and thereafter attended the Catholic cathedral a hundred yards up the street.

From the start, Lutheranism in Norway has been stagnant. During the seventeenth century it shut itself off from the broadening influences that gave it vitality in Germany. Innovation in the end took the form of pietism, which has deep roots today in the valleys of western Norway despite the efforts of the State Church first to contain and later to suppress it: the emotionalism, other worldliness and unhealthy probing into spiritual experience that it induces are a poor substitute for the old faith.

The bidding prayers followed—for the sick, the Storting, the youth of Norway. Suddenly, first three, then a huddle of sleeveless young ladies crowded the sanctuary; a mass of infants was carried in; women lined up on one side of the altar, men on the other. A parish baptism was about to begin. The pastor read a printed address on the sacrament. The Creed was recited again. The ceremony occurred at the altar rails; after it the pastor disappeared once more behind the reredos to re-emerge in a red chasuble. The preface followed, and soon he had started the consecration narrative.

The behaviour of the people was a commentary on their belief: nothing in their demeanour indicated worship of a *real* sacramental presence in the Catholic sense. The words of consecration over, they sat to a man; at communion the bread was brought out from behind the altar, the wine poured into small cups for the individual recipient. They approached devoutly, but as the first semicircle of faithful on the altar-steps made way for the second, each walked back to his pew arms swinging, as though on the first stage of his journey home. The great moment was kept to the end, when the pastor, turning to face the congregation and holding himself to his full height, chanted a long and splendid blessing, to which the congregation responded with three sung *amens*. Still in his vestments he walked to the end of the aisle and shook hands with each member of the congregation as he came out.

From start to finish a sense of mystery was lacking. The old Norse deities inspired awe; so did the Catholic rites; but this service was pedestrian. Lutheran hymns are as fine as any found in reformed churches, but they cannot replace a ritual which appeals with its rhythm and motions, even when its meaning is imperfectly understood.

This whole area, from Steinkjer to the north and west, was heavily populated in early times. Vattbaken on the northern outskirts is the site of a Stone Age village marked now by a plinth: burial mounds have been excavated all the way along the ridge to Egge church but many large barrows are still untouched. There is work of excavation here for many more archaeologists than can be put into the field.

Six kilometres to the west of Egge lies the hamlet of Bardal, and two hundred yards up the road from the water, behind a farm building, a large slab of thick slate is embedded in the hillside. On its surface there are carvings, picked out now in red and yellow paint, of different prehistoric eras: the earliest perhaps from 3000 B.C.—elks, deer, birds, whelps and bears; then, from about the year 1000 B.C., geometrical drawings and figures of men; and, most recent, but still pre-historic, high-prowed ships that have the same lines as the Viking vessels; and finally, certain unexplained circular patterns and drawings of the sun. The ships

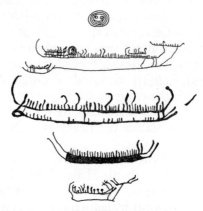

*Rock carvings at Bardal*

are steered not with a rudder but an oar, the steer or starboard. Later the Vikings added mast and sail, which they learnt from the Romans.

Near Sakshaug, twenty kilometres from Steinkjer, a ferry crosses the small strait that divides Trondheim-fjorden from Beitstadfjord, really an inlet of the former. There is no logic in the nomenclature of fjords: an arm of a main fjord often but not always has its own name; possibly this depends on its length.

From the further bank the road cuts over high ground to Leksvik, a small port developed by the Cistercian monks from the island of Tautra, which today is more easily approached from its eastern side.

Tautra was a Norwegian foundation by monks from Lysekloster near Bergen. The old monastic buildings were of timber: nothing of them remains today except the foundation walls and a section of the north wall of the adjoining stone church. It is a site of superb beauty. Many rare herbs, flowers and vegetables, brought from France, were cultivated by the monks: turnips, beans and peas are mentioned in the records, while even now a number of flowers grow wild only there—escapes from the old monastic garden. In 1644 a traveller mentions 'the beautiful apple orchard which has been planted by the monks'; in the eighteenth century an *apoteker* or chemist from Trondheim used to cross to the island to gather rare herbs.

In Catholic days the monastery was a place of pilgrimage, the spiritual focus of the district. Its end was hastened by the introduction of a Danish abbot in 1510. Vivid and probably exaggerated stories survive of his years of misrule. Among other crimes, he was reprimanded for telling ribald stories in the presence of acolytes, for disregarding fasts, striking monks during Mass and tearing the hair out of officiating priests. But at that time Norwegians dramatised stories against the Danes as they do today against the Swedes.

Beyond Leksvik a rough road follows the west bank of Trondheimfjord: it is little used even at the height of the tourist season and sheep lie asleep on sunny patches on the surface. On a day of sun and high cloud it is as glorious as any stretch of the French riviera and totally undeveloped.

This broad peninsula of hilly country is everywhere as peaceful as it must have been in the time of the monks. At Vanvikan, where a ferry crosses to Trondheim, the road turns west to the interior: it is a countryside almost insular and isolated. In the fields the peasant families were out haymaking. The method they use is peculiar to Norway. The high railing fixed to the ground is formed by upright posts to which cross-pieces are lashed with birch twig or rope. The grass is hung over the screen and dried by the wind. Corn is not stooked: the sheaves are placed above each other and a pole passed through the whole stack.

# Norway

At Rissa, about twenty kilometres inland, a turn to the further coast leads to the ruins of Reinskloster, a monastery for women founded in 1226. From its first years the community was aristocratic and many members of the old Norwegian royal family joined it. Today only a few walls remain, part of the old church now incorporated in a fine manor house.

From the sea this shore of the fjord appears sparsely inhabited: the population lies a little inland in small valleys broad enough to get the sun for more months in the year than many places further south. For the visitor seeking a tract of essential Norway it is worth driving almost aimlessly in this old and historic area. Austråt, across Stjørnfjorden, should be seen. The manor, built by the King's Chancellor, Uve Bjølke, in 1645 has open galleries on three sides with rows of carved figures. The right wing and tower originally belonged to the medieval stone church. On the first floor is the Hall of the Knights, with their chapel below. The building achieved new

*Austråt manor*

fame when Ibsen wrote his *Lady Inger of Østråt*, set in the Norway of 1528 and described at least twice in his letters as the best of his plays. Burnt down in 1916 it is now fully and exactly restored.

# West Trøndelag

The ferry from Vanvikan (it takes about two hours) docks to the south of Munkholmen, a small island off Trondheim which in Catholic times belonged to Benedictine monks. The place has a special interest for Englishmen for it was visited in 1246 by Matthew Paris, a monk of St Albans, who was both an artist of distinction and an historian of his times comparable in importance to St Bede. Matthew Paris and Henry III of England shared a common friendship with Håkon IV of Norway. When a fraudulent abbot happened to impoverish Munkholmen and abscond with the convent seal the English monk raised a loan in London to rescue the monastery. Later a new abbot fell foul of the Archbishop of Trondheim, but it was eventually agreed between them that both should petition the Pope for Matthew Paris to act as peacemaker. Innocent IV agreed. It is a great loss to Norway that Paris left no sketches of the country during his visit that lasted a little less than a year. Nor does he say much about his journey except that he narrowly escaped death during Mass at Bergen when lightning struck the ship in which he had sailed from England; before the return voyage King Håkon replaced the splintered mast of Matthew's ship and gave him rich cloths to take back to his monastery of St Albans. The most enduring result of his stay was the impulse he gave to Norwegian painting in the style of his own monastic school. Today Munkholmen is a popular bathing resort for the youth of Trondheim.

# CHAPTER 14
# THE THREE VALLEYS-
# KONGSBERG-TELEMARK

*I have used a few stories and descriptions from Telemark
to write some short poems.*
Henrik Ibsen to Schulerud, 5 January 1850

The road from Trondheim, when it reaches Støren,
fifty-one kilometres south, gives a choice of three
valleys back to Oslo. The principal road continues over
Dovrefjell through Dombås and Otta down Gudbrandsdalen; to the east there is a fork to Røros, and from there
two parallel valleys run south, through Østerdal and
nearer to the Swedish border through Trysil: the last
two are in fact a series of valleys rather than a single
grand valley like the first.

Dovrefjell is dreary or grand according to your mood.
It separates south Trøndelag from Gudbrandsdalen;
in places it rises to 3,300 feet. At Drivstua, Kongsvoll
and Fokstua there are inns, the successors of the Dovre
shelters that existed in saga times. In 1120 King
Eystein provided property to maintain these refuges;
later they were taken over by the Church, then, after
the Reformation, given to farmers on condition that
they kept the hostelries and provided pack-horses for
travellers.

At the verge of the road over the mountains, here and
on all high passes, staves are planted in the ground to
point the route in winter. It is a custom going back for
centuries: at the end of the winter they mark the trail
for snowploughs. There is grand scenery to both west
and east, fantastically shaped rocks and distant glaciers.

Earlier I had travelled through Gudbrandsdalen
and Østerdal: only the Trysil valley was unexplored;
therefore at Støren I took the road that follows the River

# The Three Valleys

Gaula to the mountain town of Røros. It is a pleasing drive mostly through farming country, climbing up to a high exposed plain: along the road there are many old farmsteads with turf roofs set against a background of forest.

As with Mo i Rana the foundation of Røros can be dated exactly. It came into existence in 1644 with the discovery of its copper: the Thirty Years War led to the quick development of the mines. Yet in spite of the mining that goes on still, Røros is one of the most pleasant towns in Norway, slightly conscious of its tourist attraction, old by Norwegian reckoning, for it was last

*Røros*

burnt down in the seventeenth century. Most of the houses date from this time and run in two parallel streets up a steep hill: built originally for rich merchants, there is no finer grouping of old town houses in Norway

with their decorative portals, window-casings and
high-gabled roofs. Behind are barns and pens: the
winter temperature here is often 40 degrees below zero
and sheep and cattle live across the yard from their
owners, sometimes till late in May.

The only important brick building in Røros is the
baroque church (there is one other in Norway at
Kongsberg) high up the hill in the main street. A series
of portraits of mine owners, managers, merchants and
worthies, many of them with German names, provide
a personal history of the town. The undoubted charm
of the place is enhanced by the starkness of the countryside: little grows, but there are moderate pastures.

Johan Petter Falkberget, the Norwegian novelist and
poet, an old man, lived here. His father was a miner of
Røros. Like his surroundings his style is rugged. He
belonged to the grand generation of Sigrid Undset and
had made Røros his special domain as Undset did
Gudbrandsdalen. He was too sick to receive me.[1]

At Os, less than half an hour's drive south from
Røros, I turned east to the Trysil valley: the main
road, however, continues south into Østerdal. For speed
and for trout fishing the Østerdal route is to be recommended. It follows the Glomma, Norway's longest
river, passes through Tynset and down the valley on the
east side of the almost impassable mountain range over
which Gudbrandsdalen lies. Lakes and forests alternate
or mingle: half way to Elverum at the end of the valley
is Rendal, where tracks to the west lead into the hills
and to some of the finest panoramic views in all
Norway.

The road nearer the Swedish border is the least used
of the three routes south, but it has a quiet appeal all
its own, similar to the Swedish uplands with their hill
farms, isolated lakes and forests of fir.

The historian can trace here the old track from
Sarna across the Swedish border to St Olav's shrine at

[1] Johan Falkberget died at Røros in 1967.

# The Three Valleys

Trondheim: medieval pilgrims were the prayerful precursors of the modern tourists in their Volvos. When the shrine of St Olav was demolished, the paths fell into disuse. Even the main artery from the south up Gudbrandsdalen, which Norwegian pilgrims followed, was barely traceable in the eighteenth century. Malthus wrote of his journey from Oslo to Trondheim in 1799: 'We were surprised to find many parts of the road almost covered with grass and very little used.' Wars between Norway and Sweden had kept the road in good condition in the early part of the century, but it had not been needed for military purposes for sixty years; people on business travelled to Trondheim by sea and in the smaller valleys of Østerdal and Trysil the old paths to Trondheim disappeared almost without trace.

Trysil is a quiet place with a reasonable hotel. A few miles to the south of the town a broad road runs east to west, connecting the three valleys, passing through Elverum at the south end of Østerdal, and on to Hamar. When completed, it will be the fastest highway between Sweden and Norway.

Culturally Norway, in the south, looks towards Denmark, in the west towards the Netherlands and England; this road may in time serve to increase the mutual influence between Sweden and Norway. Except as tourists, Swedes are seldom seen in Norway; only on the southern border is inter-marriage between the two nations common. The popular belief is that the Swedes are more formal, but this is a superficial difference; once their formality cracks they are uninhibited. Even before industrialisation, they had been wealthier; they are more Teutonic in their application to work, more business-like, organised and dominating; they produce philosophers, film-stars and fine steel, while the Norwegians paint, fish, talk and sail.

The new broad road from Trysil over Kjernberget to Elverum and Hamar will bring more Swedish visitors to Norway and the reverse traffic will increase.

# Norway

Thanks to the Nordic Council (*Nordisk Råd*) a number of Inter-Scandinavian enterprises have been established and cultural exchanges—theatre, opera and ballet—are now frequent. There is also much industrial cooperation, particularly in shipping, architecture, engineering and design.

It was in the area between Trysil and Elverum that an attempt was made in April 1940, first to capture and then to bomb King Håkon and Crown Prince Olav. Elverum today is well known to Norwegians because it was here that the King rejected the German demand for a puppet government led by Quisling. The King's 'No' is commemorated by a stone memorial. After this rejection Håkon was pursued towards Trysil by German bombers. Near Midskog (mid-forest), between these two places, there was a skirmish on 9 April 1940 when a German platoon out to capture the King was forced to withdraw by Norwegian guerrillas. When in 1967 an open competition was announced for a statue of Håkon for a site near the waterfront in Oslo, several entrants took as their subject the King sheltering in this forest from German dive-bombers. Håkon under the Norwegian fir has become an historical legend in Norway, comparable to Alfred and the burnt cakes, or Bruce and the spider: the incident, however, is well grounded in fact.

From Hamar I made a cross-country journey in a south-westerly direction to the town of Kongsberg. In early August there was already a chill in the air. The ferry from Hamar cut across the middle of Mjøsa to Kapp; from there a road crossed some high ground to strike the route south from Lillehammer via Gjøvik and Hønefoss to Oslo, a pleasant alternative to the more frequented road via Hamar. In the early stages south it follows Lake Einevatn, then zigzags over a forested mountain down to Brandbu and on to Hønefoss.

Gran near Brandbu on Granvollen is worth a visit. An old halt on the pilgrim route to Trondheim, it has

# Kongsberg

'sister' churches less than a hundred yards apart. The guidebooks' explanation that they were built by two sisters is mere supposition; more likely, one was the parish church, the other the chapel of the grange belonging to the Cistercian monks of Hovedøya, Oslo; but this is speculation. Only in Norway, with its scant historical records, is such a riddle possible.

There are other mysteries in several places on this ridge, Granvollen. A few hundred yards from the twin churches there are the remains of the only stone domestic building to survive from the Middle Ages. Again, its origin is a matter of conjecture. The first floor consists of a square hall leading into a banqueting or living-room. Possibly it was an episcopal or royal residence, possibly a resting place for pilgrims. A few kilometres in the opposite direction from Gran, on the same ridge, there are several rune stones in the church-yard of Sandkirke: a Norwegian friend, passing his fingers along the rim of carvings, interpreted them for me. As in western Somerset, the feeling of a mystical past shrouds these hills.

Hønefoss, a short cross-country drive from Brandbu, is the junction of roads that lead to lovely country in all directions. A broad waterfall through the centre of the town is spoilt by a background of chimneys. Posters advertised a travelling exhibition of the drawings of the Norwegian artist Sørensen. On the opening day I found blank walls: the pictures had been mislaid in transit. There is a Catholic chapel here with an unusual *preste-gård*: the upper floor, a bed-sitting room, was once a hen-house, the basement dining-room a pig-pen.

The principal road between Oslo and Bergen passes through Hønefoss. It follows the route of the railway up Hallingdal to Geilo, but there is a second and more southerly road through Drammen, Kongsberg and Telemark, considered by many Norwegians more dramatic though less scenically rugged than the first.

179

I was making for Telemark and took cross-country roads to Kongsberg, on the Vågen river, at the entrance to the Province.

It is a curious and large town, mildly decayed in glory. In the early nineteenth century it was still the largest town after Bergen. There were many irregular timber buildings and a church in rococo style comparable only to Røros. The interior, in fact, was more like an opera house, with a royal box facing the pulpit, flanked by other boxes for the royal entourage; the middle and merchant classes had their elevated pews on either side of the altar; the miners were relegated to the galleries a little below the roof.

This eighteenth-century church followed on the discovery of silver, but as the mines began to fail at the end of the following century, the town declined. An English traveller in 1799 observed how 'This place, like Christiania, swarms with beggars, who beset the door of the inn at which travellers arrive, forming together a mob of the most disgusting objects; each endeavouring to extort money . . . by exposing to view distorted limbs and deformity and open sores, thrusting these revolting sights in the very faces of every stranger they meet.' Today the arms industry and its subsidiaries support the town.

The mines finally closed in 1957: as they were three miles from the centre, they never disfigured the town. The main bridge over the River Lågen is decorated with statuary: a muscular youth brandishing a hammer and anvil, a popular motif with Norwegians, has a significance difficult to determine.

The women of Telemark are said to have the most striking looks of all Norwegians. It is a fact which Malthus noted on his journey through this district: 'In Sweden we had remarked that the men were much superior to the women. Here [in Kongsberg] we should make the contrary observation, and particularly among the higher classes. We [met] with many pretty elegant

looking women; but scarcely a single man that had the
air of a gentleman.' Malthus moved mainly among the
best families: but there are also young girls on the farms
of Telemark with the refined features and the natural
culture of the ancient peasants.

From Kongsberg the road into the heart of Telemark
goes over Meheia Hill down to Notodden, a town
beautifully situated but spoilt by a nitrate factory and its
chimneys, the only such total desecration I have met
in Norway. The fumes impel you westward towards
Seljord. Four kilometres out of Notodden, on the right
of the road, is Heddal stave church, the largest in
Norway. It is now partly reconstructed and, apart from
its cloisters, it has less interesting detail than many. But
only when you have reached the summit of the pass
above Nutheim and look down the grand valley of

*Flatdal*

Flatdal towards Seljord does the Telemark of travellers'
tales begin.

Here in this valley, and off it, is everything that makes
up the Norwegian peasant and national culture: a
valley of legends, song, *stabburs* or store-houses, turf-
roofed houses, mountain trolls, writers, silversmiths
and painters.

When Malthus visited Norway in 1799 he was

entertained in Oslo by Mr and Mrs Bernt Anker in their town house which was demolished to make way for the railway station on the east side; he gives an account of the ball they gave there, how they sent their linen to be washed in England, his conversation with the family, who a few decades later made their niche in Norwegian history, when the 1814 declaration of independence was signed in the house of Bernt's cousin, Karsten Anker, at Eidsvoll, between Hamar and Oslo. In the Storting there is a painting of this event. Now, a century and a half later, I was the guest of John Anker at Nutheim overlooking Flatdal and was made welcome no less kindly, but more modestly: one of his wife's forebears had been pastor of the nearby Heddal stave church.

The most crucial event in Norwegian history is the Black Death, which struck Norway more devastatingly than any other country in Europe. It entered through Bergen with the crew of an English merchantman in 1349, passed over Sognefjell into Valdres and Oppland, and then spread over all Norway from Trondheim south: from Bergen it was carried to the Faroes and Orkney, but not to Iceland or Greenland; it reached Sweden in 1350, Russia the next year. The Icelandic histories say that two-thirds of the population of Norway perished: there is a check on this calculation by the recorded drop in the returns of Peter's Pence—in the Stavanger diocese the annual sum sent to Rome was exactly two-thirds less than before the plague.

Several place-names in Telemark registered the disaster: Svartdal (black valley), Mandal (the valley of one man) and further away, in Gudbrandsdalen, the township of Tretten, where only thirteen persons were left; at Langlim, one woman with long limbs. In the deep valleys there was no escape from it; in all places the greater part of the clergy perished. In Trondheim the entire cathedral chapter was struck except for one canon; in Bergen fourteen priests and six deacons were buried on the same day. A dispensation was obtained from Rome for the ordination of clergy under the canonical age of twenty-five. In 1371, when there was a recurrence of the epidemic and Archbishop Olav died, his successor could call on only forty frail old priests in the Trondheim archdiocese, where before there had been three hundred. The shrine of St Olav was loaded with gifts and in 1350 King Magnus led a national pilgrimage there to pray for the end of the plague.

It took centuries to obliterate the memory of the plague. Tales, undoubtedly exaggerated, are told of overgrown and ruined churches discovered later in dense forests, of whole settlements depopulated, and children left alone to grow up in a wild state.

With the Black Death the old literary activity of Norway was interrupted. A century later Danish was used as the official language in purely Norwegian affairs. In the cities, and among the clergy and upper classes, Danish in a modified form took over from the vernacular: to speak Danish, even imperfectly, was a sign of culture. The change is explained by the decimation of the nobility. Only sixty out of some three hundred noble families survived the Black Death. By a curious after-effect they became incapable of bearing male children. Since by law they had to marry into their own class, the girls took foreign, mostly Danish, husbands. Consequently not only did Danish supersede Norwegian as the language in upper class speech, but by 1537 all the strong points of Norway were in Danish hands; all the members of the Royal Council were Danes except for two; as a class the Norwegian city burghers had not yet come into existence.

The country therefore was without native leadership in 1533 when the vacant throne was claimed by Prince Kristian III of Denmark, an ardent Lutheran.

The churchmen, still Norwegian, resisted in places by force but they had no influence in the Council and in the field were no match for the disciplined Danish troops. It is a shabby story. According to all its historians, Norway now reached the nadir of its history.

Telemark is rich in folklore and legends, both old and new. At Seljord at the further end of this valley, there is a statue erected to Magnus Landstad, who assembled them, as he travelled from hamlet to hamlet and was entertained, among others, by my hostess's greatgrandfather, the pastor of Heddal stave church. There are stories still in this area, mainly about pastors, now passing into folklore; for example, the old eccentric priest of Flatdal, who was the fastest man on skis in the countryside and would answer a summons to the sick or dying in a flash. His set marriage-sermon is remembered in the countryside; at a certain point he would describe the reception to follow and how, when the last guest was gone, the couple now standing before him would 'draw the blinds of their new home and enjoy heaven on earth'.

However, the local collection of tales and ballads from Telemark, like the main collection made by Asbjørnsen and Moe, belongs mainly to the time of the union with Denmark that followed the Reformation: unlike the tales of other countries, the king is a fat, genial, approachable figure who lives, not in a palace, but in a grand farm, himself a grand farmer—his home is the *kongesgård*, a collection of farm buildings flanked by outhouses; his wealth is in his fields, forests and beasts.

All through Telemark were these *gårds*, unchanged since the time of Askelad, the hero of the folktales, with their timber *stuer*, sheep-pens and store-houses: the background is the same today as then. And there is the same fear of natural forces: the sudden blizzard or fall of snow, the impenetrable mist, the cold. Every Easter, when two-thirds of the population desert the towns for the countryside, 'mountain rules' are printed in the daily papers: they are substantially the rules observed by Askelad and all should respect them. Don't set out on a ski tour unless you are in good form; don't go alone; listen to experienced mountain folk; be equipped against bad weather even on a short excursion—never forget map and compass; make it known where you are going; respect the weather and weather report; turn back in good time—there is no shame in turning; keep together in a crisis; spare your reserves of strength; seek shelter in good time; dig into the snow when necessary.

Half way down the road into the valley of Flatdal is a turning into Åmotsdal, a narrow, lesser valley of immense beauty, with old farm buildings and by-tracks,

*Detail from a painted bed at Tubås farm,*
*Heddal: Napoleon leading his army*

the summer resort of painters. Here my hosts, like the Ankers, had assembled from other parts of the country old buildings which they had refurbished as a summer residence: the type of houses seen in the open-air museums of Oslo and Lillehammer. In fact these museums have created an alertness to the historic value of ancient timbered buildings. Before continuing my journey, I visited an old *prestegård*, half-way down to valley, transferred from another place and reconstructed here: it is a museum in itself, with its painted walls, pews and ceilings. At the entrance of the valley, across the river, is a superb, intricately carved *stabbur*, a finer example than I had seen in any museum.

It is possible to date these buildings by their timber. In the eighteenth century mountain pine was preferred because it grew slowly: to make it more durable, the branches were lopped off a year before it was felled and a boulder placed on the top. In this way the sap was retained: the process was later discontinued.

For centuries many parts of Norway subsisted almost exclusively on timber. In the interior, where the cost of transport to the coast made it uneconomical to export planks, spars and beams, it was used to make charcoal for the glass and smelting furnaces. In the north most roads were constructed from wood: decaying trees were used to produce turpentine; ashes were converted into fertilisers. Moreover, the forest provided also the only fuel and material for building.

There is much in the valleys of Telemark that only a native can call to your notice; it is the most rewarding of all provinces for a long stay: in one place or another can be found the best examples of all that goes to constitute the true culture of Norway that is so easily missed by the modern tourist.

# CHAPTER 15
# SØRLANDET-VESTFOLD-ØSTFOLD

*I can put up with everything else but not this flirting
with the Swedes. Because of the very foundations of their
civilization the Swedes are our spiritual enemies.*
Henrik Ibsen to Magdalene Thoresen,
31 March 1868

At Seljord, at the southern end of Flatdal, the road
forks. There is a route north-west to Bergen, which
before Dalen passes within three hundred yards of a
dramatic ravine that drops vertically into the valley,
forming a current of air that sucks into it any light
object placed near the edge; further on, the route
ascends to a mountain *vidda*, where snow is several feet
thick even in July, and continues via Odda to Bergen.
In the early part of this drive two places of special
interest are worth a halt: the eighteenth-century church
at Vinje where there are paintings by Henrik Sørensen
and, before the ascent to Odda begins at Breifonn, the
stave church at Røldal. The wooden crucifix above the
chancel beam here was believed to be miraculous in the
Middle Ages and was the object of pilgrimages long
after Catholic times.

The other prong of the Seljord fork turns directly
south and hits the coast near Tvedestrand about ten
miles east of Arendal. This road that follows the lakes
to Åmli is as lovely as any other section of Telemark: at
Åmli it again forks, south-west to Kristiansand, south-
east to Arendal.

Sørlandet is the name given to the southern coast of
Norway: like Vestlandet, it has no rigidly defined limits,
but it can be taken to extend the length of the northern
side of the Skagerrak from Farsund to Kragerø. Here on

the coast and the innumerable islands, isolated and in clusters, wooded, rocky, bare-backed and fertile, the Norwegians have their small houses or bungalows where they live the greater part of the summer. The long hours of June sunshine bring the sea to a higher temperature than in England. In places the coast is as attractive as any

*South coast scene*

in Europe; its pure light, particularly in the late evening, has always appealed to Norwegian painters, many of whom spend their summer months there; however, the immediate hinterland is plain in comparison with the rest of Norway, though there are some sites of historical interest. The main valleys leading into the interior are impressive, and the coastal road from Mandal to Oslo, a six-hour drive, is beautiful in parts. This is not the Norway of the tourist offices. In summer it is left to the Norwegians from Oslo, in winter to the residents— the bungalows are then shut, the beaches deserted, the quaysides empty. It can be visited by sea on the cargo boats that sail regularly from Oslo to Kristiansand and call with mail and goods at all the small ports: in spring and early summer there are folk dances sometimes on the waterfronts on Saturday evening.

There is a gaiety peculiar to these southerners, a race very different from the people of the interior. The explanation is perhaps that this coast was favoured by the Danes in the seventeenth century. Kristiansand

itself was founded by King Kristian IV of Denmark in
1641, but in spite of its privileges, it never became, as he
had planned it, the great capital of the south: it has fine
houses, some interesting buildings (like the old theatre
no longer in use), broad streets and a long waterfront,
yet it remains a dull plain place. To the south is Mandal,
with the finest bathing beaches in the country, and to
the north is Setesdal, which is exaggeratedly praised by
the guide-books. Its inhabitants are said to be descendants of the Scots who came over in the fourteenth
century to replace the people who had died in the
plague: they are believed to be dour in an un-Norwegian
way. The valley follows the River Ostra up from
Kristiansand, through Bylke, into the mountains and so
across to Haugesund or Bergen. The ferry which now
connects Kristiansand with Harwich makes this a
pleasant way of starting an exploration of Norway.

Often in the villages of these high valleys like
Setesdal flags are seen flying at half-mast from almost
every farmstead, a last tribute to a member of the
community who is being buried that day. Customarily
the entire village is present in the church; programmes
of hymns are printed and all join in the service, in
winter coming on their skis and sledges. It is a moving
ceremony. After the interment the chief mourners meet
for sandwiches, coffee and comment on the panegyric
made by the pastor.

In cities the funerals are less sincere: the cremation
may account partly for the difference. The smart
families engage the best-known preachers, who are
often hard put to it to praise an old deceased gentleman
they had never set eyes on. Professional choristers are
engaged by the undertaker: they sing the traditional
hymns at the graveside and, at their conclusion, are
occasionally seen to wipe their tears, lick their fingers
and count their ten kroner notes. In springtime it is
inadvisable for lady mourners to wear floral hats; the
undertakers are brisk and likely to mistake them for

wreaths: it can happen that the hats are last seen adorning the coffin as it slides into the furnace. After a funeral in Oslo the family assemble for what the Norwegians call bluntly *gravmat* and *gravøl*, literally grave-food and grave-beer.

To the north of Kristiansand the main towns of Sørlandet are Arendal, Larvik and Sandefjord: between them lie a number of delightful small ports and fishing villages like Tvedestrand, Risør, Kragerø, Langesund, Brevik and Stavern.

Tvedestrand, a fishing hamlet built on a steep hill running down to the sea, had the distinction of maintaining the last town watchman in Norway. The task of these men was to walk the streets at night until 4 a.m., give warning of fire, care for the street lights, call out the time and the direction of the wind and to sing their song. Their livery consisted of a long red cape, a leather cap and a belt on which the words *Faithful and True* were embroidered in letters of gold. In their hand they carried a spiked pole, their *morgensterne* (morning star) for their protection

Until 1968 the night watchman of Tvedestrand walked the streets in silence. There are old people in the town who remember when he still sang his song in his metallic voice:

> *Hark to the town watchman!*
> *The clock is striking ten.*
> *Now is the time to go to bed.*
> *The housewife and her maid,*
> *The master and his man.*
> *The wind is south-south-east.*

Sometimes in winter he would call out, 'The clock is striking . . . ,', slip on the icy pavement and, after a long pause, add 'ten'.

In Oslo the last night watchman disappeared from the streets in 1858, in Bergen in 1874. When the last holder

of the office in Tvedestrand retired recently the rate-
payers declined to maintain a successor.

There is little left of the faded past of Arendal, once
Norway's busiest seaport; in summer the sound is full
of sailing boats, and the streets crowded with visitors.
Larvik has a ferry across to Fredrickshavn in the north
of Jutland. Sandefjord with the neighbouring town of
Tønsberg are the old bases of the Norwegian whaling
fleet that operated first in the Arctic, then later in the
Antarctic. It was the men from Tønsberg who invented
the grenade-tipped harpoon that exploded inside the
beast and made it possible to hunt the stronger and
faster blue whale; later they designed the factory-ship
into which the whale was guided like a tourist down the
slipway of a drive-on ferry. Safely inside it was stripped
like a banana. The record year was 1930–31 when
40,200 whales were caught, half of them by Norwegians.

After the Second World War Japan and Russia entered
into competition with Norway. They refused to join the
international control organisation and began a massive
slaughter of whales. Of the giant whales only a few
hundred survived. Though still operating a few whalers,
Tønsberg switched to the tanker business; all these
coastal towns now have their shipbuilding yards. Mr
Jahre, the owner of the Park Hotel, designed by the
architect of Oslo Town Hall (it seats 1,100 in the dining-
room), still operates the Oslo–Kiel ferry, a large fleet of
tankers and one whaler in the Antarctic. His hotel is noted
for its *hval kjøtt*, the best fillet of whale to be had anywhere in the world.

Tønsberg is the oldest city in Norway. In Viking
days it was the capital. The sagas mention it more
frequently than any other place; there are still some
indications of its antiquity, for instance the foundations, recently excavated, of an old circular church in
the centre of the city and the ruins of a thirteenth-
century castle overlooking it. Many actions were
fought in the approaches and the neighbouring fjords

between the royal fleet and pirate Viking bands. The two splendid ships in the Bygdøy Museum in Oslo were found in this district: the Godstad ship from Sandefjord, the most perfect example of a Viking ship discovered anywhere in the world, and the older Oseberg ship, dating from about 800 and discovered in 1903. It is less impressive but more interesting: when it was reconstructed its timbers were still live enough to stand being bent back to their original position without cracking.

During the British blockade of Norway in the Napoleonic wars, Tønsberg was again an important naval base. The Danish-Norwegian battle fleet destroyed by Hyde Parker and Nelson at Copenhagen was quickly replaced by a flotilla of small gunboats. All along this coast they preyed on British shipping: lighthouses remained dark, buoys were misplaced, privateers ambushed from behind the skerries. To meet the loss, a large-scale convoy system was organised by the British Admiralty. Nevertheless the Danes and Norwegians seized 2,000 British merchant ships during the war. It was the last war waged by the united kingdom of Denmark and Norway.

Tønsberg is also associated with Amundsen. It was from here in September 1910 that he sailed for the South Pole in the *Fram* (now in Bygdøy) which belonged to his friend, Fridtjof Nansen.

The expedition caused much bitterness in England. Nansen, who had been rescued by a British party from an ice-floe in the Arctic many years earlier, was always pro-British. When Norwegian Minister in London, he had been invited to lead a British party to the Antarctic; later he gave advice and support to Scott. He told Scott he should use dogs and sledges with ski-runners. At the cost of many lives, Scott insisted on ponies and sledges.

Amundsen was a Norwegian of different temper from Nansen. He inherited Nansen's ship and plans, but not his unselfishness in research. Between 1908 and 1911 he was working in Bergen on the scientific data provided by Nansen's two-year drift on the north Arctic pack-ice: all understood that he was preparing for another north Arctic drift. However, he was in financial difficulties; moreover, when Perry planted the

*The* Fram

American flag at the North Pole in 1909, Amundsen's projected expedition lost its appeal with the Norwegian public. He persuaded himself that he had to get to the South Pole first in order to win sufficient réclame to raise the necessary cash for a north Arctic exploration. Nansen commented that it was a strange thing to go to the North Pole via the South Pole.

In fact, it was only after Amundsen was at Madeira that Nansen learned that his friend had sailed for the Antarctic. He kept his plan secret even from his crew until he reached the open sea. With his dogs and ski-sledges he arrived at the South Pole on 15 December 1911, a year after leaving Tønsberg and five weeks before Scott with his ponies. He was hailed as a hero. Nansen, who never approved of Amundsen's competitiveness, was distressed at a letter he received from him south of Madeira, saying that he 'was going to fight the English to the South Pole'. In England there were fierce recriminations against Amundsen who finally on 12 May 1926 reached the North Pole in the airship *Norge*. He died two years later in an attempt to rescue the Italian, Nobile, wrecked in the same region in another airship, the *Italia*.

Tønsberg, Tromsø and other places have their statues of Amundsen. Understandably he became a hero of Norwegian youth. He appears never to have grown up from boyhood: his failings and virtues were those of the schoolboy. Nansen, on the other hand, by reason of his world vision and philanthropic work established a claim to be considered one of the greatest Europeans of this century.

Between Tønsberg and Oslo (the district is called Vestfold) lies Horten with its fine yacht harbour: it is the Cowes of Norway and the June regatta is a sight tourists invariably miss. Further on, Drammen is a growing industrial town that no motorist can avoid if he returns to Oslo from the south or west. It has a curious attraction in the *Spiralen*, a long tunnel cut through the interior of the hill overlooking the town and cork-screwing for a mile inside the rock to emerge on a plateau that gives a view of the fjord and the intersection of several valleys. The prison in the town is very fashionable and much sought after by women who have to serve twenty-one days for driving offences. It provides double rooms, good food and opportunities for exercise and reading. It is said that the inhabitants of Drammen are solid citizens who despise the people of Oslo as money-makers of a wicked metropolis. Drammensveien back into Oslo in the height of summer has worse traffic than Piccadilly.

Some of the best farmland in Norway is in Østfold, the district to the east side of Oslofjord. Few tourists visit it. Swedes and Danes driving north from Gothenburg seldom leave the main highway, Englishmen, coming mostly via Bergen, scarcely know the area. It extends to the Swedish border in the east and south; in the region of Lake Øyeren and to the west, near Fredrikstad, it contains broad stretches of rich undulating farmland.

Driving south from Oslo, Moss, an industrial and shipbuilding centre, should be avoided, though there is a convenient ferry joining it with Horten on the other shore of the fjord. Drøbak on the narrowest point of Oslofjord is worth a detour. It is built on a hill and has a village life uncontaminated by the capital. It is a refuge of writers and artists and has a Danish style church and many fine houses. In flatter surroundings it could be taken for a Jutland town. It was the Norwegian shore batteries on a near-by hill that on 9 April 1940 sank the German cruiser *Blücher* which was forcing its way up the fjord with all the German personnel that was to take over the civil administration of Norway for the Nazis.

Fredrikstad, lying half an hour's drive from the main route south, has an individuality as a city comparable to Bergen's. Actually Fredrikstad is two towns separated by the Glomma that rises in the hills behind Røros and flows out here into the Skagerrak: there is much old in the new town, little new in the old, and the bridge connecting them is in harmony with both.

Several retired French sea-captains settled in the new town in the eighteenth century: their influence is traceable in the fine vistas and parks as well as in the architecture, and two streets are named after them; in fact the French community was large enough to support its own priest, who lived here secretly at a time when Catholicism was still proscribed by the law. Modern developments have not spoilt the town.

The old town to the south of the Glomma is a show-piece. The ancient wooden drawbridge at its entrance is still intact and along the river front the line of its old ramparts is easily traceable. The red brick barracks, built in 1783, is one of the finest buildings in

Norway. Transplanted into an English countryside it would pass as a noble Georgian residence. The onion-towered semi-baroque church alongside hardly belongs to Norway, though it is reminiscent of the Lutheran Cathedral in Oslo. It has a fine balcony, supported by wooden Corinthian pillars. Like all Norwegian churches, it is spotless. The portraits of the nineteenth-century pastors, that customarily hang in the sacristy, are worth inspection.

Glass-blowing is the oldest industry in Fredrikstad. Close to the drawbridge is a small factory, which also provides shelter from the cold winds that often blow through the town. The design is good: and there is a range of narrow-necked vases which Norwegians use for the single rose or tulip that decorates their table in the winter months. The textiles woven here are among the most attractive in Norway.

The road south-east out of Fredrikstad back to the main north–south artery runs through the oldest part of Norway. In a stretch of ten miles or less there are in four places, by the road or a little off it, stone-age carvings similar to those near Steinkjer picked out in red on the flat rock face: figures of men, circular symbols and long-ships with a numerous crew. It has always been the country of seafaring men and farmers.

By contrast with Fredrikstad Halden is disappointing. It lies on the Swedish border. Some timbered side-streets are attractive; it also has the oldest theatre in Norway, no longer in use, a long building that looks like a warehouse.

In the eighteenth century its position gave it an importance which it has now lost. Several times it was defended successfully against the Swedes. On the hills to the south-east of the town are the ruins of the massive Norwegian fortress of Fredrikssten. From its heights cannon balls were rained into Sweden. An iron obelisk commemorates the demise of Charles XII of Sweden on this spot. The view from here over Svinesund is superb even on an overcast day.

From Halden there are two routes into Sweden. The main road crosses Svinesund by a bridge opened after the war. The ceremony was performed by King Gustav of Sweden and it was planned that he should be met half-way across by King Håkon of Norway, but at the time the Norwegian people were in no mood for such a gesture. A good secondary road runs south along Iddefjord on the Norwegian side for twenty-three kilometres before it crosses into Sweden at Holtet. It has the Norwegian scenic beauty that contrasts with the dullness of the main Swedish road. The Norwegians of this area, unlike most frontier zones, have mixed loyalties; intermarriage with Swedes, almost unknown elsewhere, is common and there is an admiration and envy of the higher standard of Swedish living. Patriotism, vibrant in all other parts of Norway, is somnolent in this lovely countryside.

Strømstad on the coast is the first place of any importance inside Sweden: a pleasant summer resort with a fan-like spread of skerries. In the Stadshotel there is a mural representing an uneven battle between Swedes and Norwegians. The Swedish soldiery stand upright to a man; the worst any Swedish musketeer suffers is the loss of his cocked hat; the Norwegians are knocked down like ninepins. It represents a scientific rather than a moral superiority.

# CHAPTER 16
# NORTH OF THE NORTH CAPE

*Praise the fineness of the day when it is ended; the ice when once you have crossed it; and the liquor after it is drunk.*

Norwegian Proverb

Spitzbergen, two days' sailing from the North Cape, comprises a series of islands allocated to Norway by international treaty in 1925. Only in an exceptional summer can it be circumnavigated; in most years its northern stretches are permanently contiguous with the north polar icefield.

In winter there is a monthly plane from Tromsø that lands on the frozen upper reaches of Adventfjord in the centre of the main island; from June to November there are coal boats from the ports of north Norway and certain tourist liners take in Spitzbergen on a round cruise. Occasionally a small luxury boat sails from Tromsø, feasts its score of passengers on caviare, guarantees each a polar bear and charges close on a thousand pounds per person. The bears are shot from the boat's deck: the skins that fetch a hundred and fifty pounds in winter are worthless in summer.

The *Ingertre*, built at Fredrikstad in 1954 and under charter to the Store Norske Kulkompani, with offices in Bergen, uses the quay on the northern side of the fjord at Mo i Rana. She is usually full of miners and their families returning from their summer leave. Others can get a berth only by arrangement with the Coal Company.

The first mention of Spitzbergen is in the Icelandic sagas as far back as 1194. From Langanes on the north-east coast of Iceland it was then reckoned four days' sailing 'to these northernmost limits of the ocean'. Today, from Mo i Rana, the geographical centre of Norway, the *Ingertre*, specially strengthened against pack-ice, took exactly the same time. Sailing in the late evening she skirted about 11 o'clock the next morning the hundred desolate islands and rocks that form the tapering end of the Lofoten islands, the last landfall before the ice-covered mountains of Svalbard, the Norwegian name for Spitzbergen. Twenty-four hours later the North Cape lay about a hundred miles to starboard; to the north-east was Bear Island, with seven hundred lakes on its northern plateaus, uninhabited except for the staff of a meteorological station; though comparatively mild in climate, it is seldom visited even by explorers.

For two days in the north Arctic no boat was sighted. In the early morning of the fourth day the white peaks of Spitzbergen could be seen through binoculars from the bridge. Ahead was the twenty-mile opening into Isfjord for which the *Ingertre* was making. Snow and sunshine alternated. The waters were the deep grey that only melting ice can produce.

The land mass was protected by a frozen sea. At 9.48 a message was received from Spitzbergen that there was ice for twenty miles off the coast. The captain plotted a provisional course. It was his second visit this year. Ten days earlier he had a clear passage; now a change of wind to the north-west had driven the floating ice from the ocean back into the fjord mouth. Once at the end of May he had been stuck in these waters for three and a half days; a sea that had been open for several days could be blocked again in the space of half an hour.

For four hours the *Ingertre* crunched slowly through the ice broken into curious shapes—mushrooms, camels, four-legged beasts floating on their backs, ducks, perfectly formed swans—all nine-tenths submerged and shining like transparent emerald below the surface.

Here and there on a more level floe a seal floated by. The polar bears had already moved south on the first drifts to spend a short summer on Bear Island; when the ocean froze again they would pad back to Svalbard and the polar fox would have the island to itself.

At midday the *Ingertre* was still searching for an opening. From the bridge I could see another ship approaching Isfjord from the east. Later a signal was received. It was a Russian coal boat reporting that conditions were better nearer land and that the fjord itself was clear of ice.

Isfjord runs deep into the centre of the main island of the Spitzbergen archipelago. Along its eastern shore are two Russian mining settlements, at Barentsburg on Grønfjord, a tributary of Isfjord, and at Grumantbyen; there is a third higher up at Pyraminden on Billefjord. The Russians were mining here before 1920, when Spitzbergen was literally no-man's-land; under the Paris treaty they were granted concessions, and although their mining operations were of little importance, the settlements remained open. From a mile out in the fjord only a collection of huts could be seen and an overhead bucket-rail running up into the mountains. The first mate passed me his glasses: 'The tunnel openings are up there', he said, telling me where to focus, 'and who knows what the Russians have got inside.'

Less than ten miles further up was the principal mining town, Longyearby, on an inlet named Adventfjord. I imagined that the place got its name from the slow passage of time in this extremity of the globe, which suffered so many days of total light and total darkness; in fact, it derived from John Munro Longyear, an American mine-owner from Marquette who formed the Arctic Coal Company of Boston and raised the first buildings here in 1906. Ten years afterwards the property was purchased by the Spitzbergen Coal Company. It resembled a mid-western township in the sixties of the last century. According to the season its population fluctuated between 800 and 1,200 persons. None was over sixty-five; deaths averaged one a year; the old folk retired to Norway.

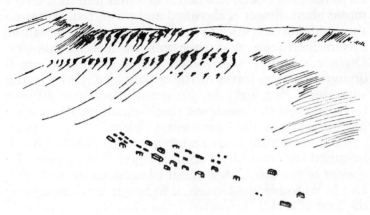

*Longyearby, Spitzbergen*

The *Ingertre* tied up at a wooden pier. A cluster of residents was gathered to meet returning relatives or receive shipments of goods ordered from the mainland. I looked out onto the sprawling capital wondering where I could lodge. Then a gentleman boarded the ship, introduced himself and explained that he had instructions from Bergen to take care of me during my stay. He was one of the three 'chiefs' of the Coal Company, a Dane, with an Austrian wife.

The same evening we walked along the edge of Adventfjord in the night sunshine, in the direction of the Russian settlement. An icy breeze, unbroken by any trees or vegetation, blew down from the glaciers on both sides of the water. The tallest plant to grow here was the dwarf birch, three to five inches high; but underfoot on soft, almost peat-like ground, just eleven degrees from the North Pole, was a mass of diminutive flowers, deep and bright in colour, and patches of scurvy-grass, a plant with white flowers, used either fresh, dried or boiled with soup, as a protection against Arctic diseases. Only in these low-lying coastal strips does the snow disappear altogether; but even here the earth remains frozen to a depth of a hundred feet. Every moss, plant, flower is classified and protected. Not even the residents can pluck them. They survive from a time, fifty million years ago, when this was a fertile country. On my return I was shown a box of fossils: small oranges, berries, leaves of full-grown birch; even in the snowstorm that was now gathering it was not difficult to believe on this evidence that Spitzbergen had once been as warm as the Continental riviera.

Except for wild dogs and fish everything that lived, breathed or moved in Spitzbergen was under the shelter of the law. A few small indigenous deer existed, and I was to see musk-oxen, standing in a group against the foot of a cliff: imported from Greenland to provide a little more life on the island, they are shy, shaggy beasts, huddling pathetically together in the patches of sun in the summer months. The wild dog is the curse of Spitzbergen: bred from the domestic dogs left behind when the whole population, Norwegian and Russian, was evacuated in September 1941, it attacks deer and men and there is a reward of a hundred shillings for shooting one.

There can be few so sparsely inhabited stretches of the earth that have more place-names than Spitzbergen: they indicate the position of a place, describe the scenery, give warning of navigational hazards, or are associated with plant or animal life or with nations and their explorers. Others like Misery Mount or Point Welcome register an experience; a few, for instance Devil's Thumb, have a religious significance. The Scots perhaps were busier here than any other people, and it is odd to find in this territory under Norwegian sovereignty Camp Morton, a group of four huts on the north shore of Mijenfjord called after the Earl of

Morton who visited Spitzbergen in 1906. The activity
of others is recorded in places like Campbellbryggen
(-wharf) and Brucebreen (-glacier). Dr William Spier
Bruce was a member of nine expeditions to Spitzbergen between 1898 and 1920, and the leader of the
Scottish Polar Expedition. Adventfjord, on which
Longyearby lay, had no association with the liturgical
season; it recalled the shipwreck of the English whaler,
*Adventure*, which was stationed here in 1656.

Many other names dated from the seventeenth
century, the great Spitzbergen whaling period. The
rivalry between English and Dutch led to battles but
also to the mapping of the coast, which was completed in
1710. The Dutch were first in these waters. In 1596 an
expedition under Willem Barents rediscovered this
land in an attempt to find the North East Passage to
China; the English under Hudson followed in 1607:
for more than a century they perversely maintained
that it was part of Greenland in which they had been
granted concessions—Nelson's visit as a midshipman
on a naval research vessel belongs to this period. The
rivalry died only in the nineteenth century with the near
extinction of the Greenland whale: Russian trappers
succeeded, in search of seals, walrus, bear, the polar
fox and reindeer. Mining was introduced in 1898.

The residents of Longyearby were all connected with
coal. The morning after my arrival I was invited to go
*up* a mine: there are no shafts, all the seams running
horizontally near the summit of the mountains. The
truck that took me to Mine 5 raced up a mud road to
the head of the fjord, then climbed into the snow. The
weather now was like mid-winter on the Norwegian
mainland. With woollen underclothes and woollen
shirt, two sweaters, jersey and overalls, I was still cold
when I stepped into the opening. For the first three
hundred yards the floor was a layer of ice; humped up,
I continued for twenty minutes, then waited while my
guide returned to fetch an hydraulic truck to take us

further in. For half an hour alone, leaning in cold and discomfort against the damp walls of the unlit lane, I tried to appreciate that I was deep inside what geologists call an aboriginal mountain, which they reckon at least six milliard years old. Eventually we drove on into a seam that was being worked with up-to-date American machinery.

These miners came mainly from northern Norway, many from Narvik and Tromsø, giants of men, bachelors for the most part, on contracts for a period of three to five years. The rhythm of their life is unique among manual labourers. They prefer winter to summer because of the deep isolation that settles on their encampments: winter (they explained to me) is always winter, but summer is a season that may pass before it has come.

Apart from the Norwegian Governor or *Sysselman* whose office is a sinecure, the entire community is in the employment of the Coal Company: it maintains the roads, the hospital, the barrack-like lodgings, the telegraphs and communications, the piers, stores, recreation hall, church and night-club. There are material compensations. Income tax stands at four per cent, a bottle of Bordeaux, priced at fourteen shillings in Oslo, can be had for two shillings, all spirits and cigarettes are tax free, wages are high, leave generous; with no family or home and little entertainment most miners work overtime. A troublesome man has his contract revoked and is compelled to return to Norway. All the miners I met calculated the period of their sojourn not by years, but by winters.

Some hunted the polar bear, found in winter even in the near neighbourhood of Longyearby: unlike the brown bear of the mainland, it does not hibernate. But the best hunting-ground is the island of Håpen, south-east of Edgeøya, which fog and swell make near inaccessible. It has been established that they gather there on the high mountain plateaus, but for the most part their movements, even their numbers, are largely guesswork. It is unsporting to shoot a bear from under a hundred and fifty yards, and there is a law, impossible of enforcement, forbidding chase from the motor-scooters which have recently become popular for excursions among the glaciers.

*Polar bears*

Trappers abound. They come from all nations for a single season or for several; they live solitarily in huts at the foot of the glaciers, they require no passport for entry or permit for the export of bear skins or walrus tusks. Shortly before my visit the skeleton of a trapper had been discovered: he had been killed by a bear in 1954; his gun had failed to fire and his bones were scattered over several acres of ice.

Skiing continues to mid-June or later; but a man racing down a lonely slope in July leaves a trail of slosh behind him. In high summer a species of polar salmon called red char can be caught in the mountain lakes near Longyearby. The Lutheran pastor, formerly a taxi-driver in Oslo, was a keen sportsman: he had killed more than one wild dog and was determined to shoot a bear before his term of service at Longyearby was over

the following spring. Already in mid-June he was count-
ing the days to the opening of the shooting season: he had
laid his plans for a five-day scooter expedition to Hal-
månøya (Half-moon Island), south-east of Longyearby.
He was also something of a casuist: the natural duty of
self-defence overrode the positive law against shooting
from a scooter, and confronted with a bear he alone was
the judge of his own peril. He explained to me the importance of selecting the right terrain for the assault: a bear
could overtake him on level ground, but he could always
outstrip it on a slope.

The church stood on an eminence overlooking the
town, which had grown up near the first mine to be
worked and was now scattered in four or five clusters of
wooden buildings. It was featureless and lacking a
centre, the disparate communities tending to lead their
own lives within the area. Two or three times a year
visits were exchanged with the nearest Russian township and there would be football matches and dances,
but the Russians mainly went their own way; the only
complaint the Longyearby people had against them was
that when they went trapping they would exhaust the
supplies of food in the huts without replenishing them.
No one could explain satisfactorily why they were there.

The only other settlement of any size is at Ny
Ålesund on the west coast, five days from Longyearby
with dogs and sledge. A small mining centre with three
to four hundred inhabitants, it was Amundsen's base
when he flew to the rescue of the Italian airship
wrecked near the North Pole—a wing of his airplane
was eventually washed up near the town. There was
once an hotel here, but it closed at the end of its first
season. Tourist ships call, and the place is now likely
to develop as an international tracking station for
satellites. Further north off the mainland is Danskøya.
On 11 July 1897 a Swede called Andrée set out from
there by balloon in an attempt to reach the North Pole
and was last seen drifting north-north-east.

# North of the North Cape

Was this archipelago of islands, frozen together in winter, a country? Perhaps it was inhabited sixty million years ago. In the summer of 1960 the footprints of a monster reptile were discovered in the rock. Could it have lived before the creation of man?

The *Ingertre* sailed at two in the morning. The snowstorm had blown itself out and the night sunlight enhanced the lucidity of the air. I felt the deep silence that fills the voids between the glaciers. During two days I had experienced some of the contrasts of the place, particularly the noise of gales and the abrupt stillness; but it was necessary to winter here to appreciate fully the darkness and light of the Arctic, its crystal atmosphere and mists, its summers and long winters under the northern lights.

If the Russians agree to the construction of an airport, Spitzbergen will lose some of its mystery. At present a step ladder on the fringe of the fjord marks the spot where the plane from Tromsø glides to a halt on the winter ice. It looked forlorn now like an abandoned diving-stage. Spitzbergen was still a desolate corner of the earth and largely insulated from the tourist traffic by a frozen sea.

# APPENDIX I
# BIBLIOGRAPHY

The purpose of this bibliography is twofold. First, to give the background of my reading for this book; secondly, to provide a hand-list for the visitor who may wish to read more fully on certain subjects that I have merely touched on. All small popular handbooks have been omitted and also books in Norwegian not available in English. Erling Grønland of the Royal University Library, Oslo, in his *Norway in English* (1961) gives a complete list of books on Norway and by Norwegians in English published between 1936 to 1959. It includes also a survey of Norwegian literature in English translation from 1742 to 1959.

BERNARD, M. R., *Sketches of Life, Scenery and Sport in Norway* (London, 1871).

BRØNSTED, JOHANNES, *The Vikings* (Penguin, 1965).

CAMPBELL, JOHN R., *How to See Norway* (Longmans, 1871).

CHRISTIANSEN, REIDAR TH., *Folktales of Norway* (Routledge, 1964).

CLARKE, E. D., *Travels*, vol. 10 (London, 1824).

CONNERY, DONALD, *The Scandinavians* (Eyre & Spottiswoode, 1966).

COXE, WILLIAM, *Travels*, vol. 5 (London, 1802).

DERRY, T. K., *The Campaign in Norway* (H.M. Stationery Office, 1952).

DERRY, T. K., *A Short History of Norway* (Allen & Unwin, 1957).

DOWNS, BRIAN W., *Modern Norwegian Literature, 1860–1918* (Cambridge, 1966).

ECKSTEIN, HARRY, *Division and Cohesion in Democracy: A Study of Norway* (Princeton, 1966).

# Bibliography

GARSTEIN, OSKAR, *Rome and the Counter-Reformation in Scandinavia* (Oxford, 1963).

GJERSET, KNUT, *History of the Norwegian People*, 2 vols (Macmillan, New York, 1915).

GORE ALLEN, W., *Renaissance in the North: Ibsen to Undset* (Sheed & Ward, 1946).

GRØNLAND, ERLING, *Norway in English: A Bibliography* (Norwegian Universities Press, 1961).

HARGEN, ANDERS, *Rock Carvings in Norway* (Johan Grundt Tanum Forlag, Oslo, 1965).

HEYERDAHL, THOR, *The Kon-Tiki Expedition* (Penguin Books, 1966).

HUNTER, L. S. (ed.), *The Scandinavian Churches* (Faber, 1965).

HVEBERG, HARALD, *Of Gods and Giants: Norse Mythology* (Johan Grundt Tanum Forlag, Oslo, 1962).

HØYER, LIV NANSEN, *Nansen: A Family Portrait* (Longmans, 1957).

IBSEN, HENRIK, *Plays* (Penguin, 5 vols, 1950–64).

JAMES, PATRICIA (ed.), *The Travel Diaries of T. R. Malthus* (Cambridge, 1966).

KEARY, C. F., *Norway and the Norwegians* (London, 1892).

*King Harald's Saga* (Penguin, 1966).

LAING, SAMUEL, *Journal of a Residence in Norway during the years, 1834, 1835 & 1836* (Longmans, 1851).

LARSEN, KAREN, *A History of Norway* (Princeton, 1938).

LE ROUX, HUGUES, *Notes sur la Norvège* (Paris, 1895).

MANKER, ERNST, *People of Eight Seasons: The Story of the Lapps* (C. A. Watts, London, 1965).

MCTAGGART, WILLIAM BELL, *Notes on Norway and Places Elsewhere* (London, 1887).

# Norway

METCALFE, FREDERICK, *An Oxonian in Norway*, 2 vols (London, 1856).

MEYER, MICHAEL, *Henrik Ibsen: The Making of a Dramatist* (Rupert Hart-Davis, 1967).

MIDGARD, JOHN, *A Brief History of Norway* (Johan Grundt Tanum Forlag, Oslo: second edition, 1964).

*Njal's Saga* (Penguin, 1960).

*Norwegian Folk Tales* from the collection of Asbjørnsen and Moe (Dreyers, Oslo, 1960).

PONTOPPIDAN, ERIC, *The Natural History of Norway* (1755).

SNORRE, STURLUSSON, *Sagas of the Norse Kings: The Olaf Sagas* (Everyman, 1964).

SPRINCHORN, E., *Ibsen: Letters and Speeches* (MacGibbon, 1965).

STAGG, FRANK NOEL, *North Norway, The Heart of Norway, West Norway and its Fjords, East Norway and its Frontier* (Allen & Unwin, 1952–59)

TURVILLE-PETRE, E. O. G., *Myth & Religion in the North* (Weidenfeld & Nicolson, 1964).

*Vinland Sagas* (Penguin, 1965).

WILLIAMS, W. M., *Through Norway with a Knapsack* (London, 1863).

WILLIAMS, W. M., *Through Norway with Ladies* (London, 1877).

# APPENDIX II
# NORWEGIAN DATES

793 First recorded Norwegian raid on England (Lindisfarne).

851 Norwegians establish kingdom of Dublin.

c. 870 Norwegian settlement of Iceland.

872 Battle of Hafrsfjord: Norway united.

911 Rollo establishes himself in Normandy.

984 Norwegian settlement of Greenland.

955 Olav Tryggvesson introduces Christianity.

1014 Battle of Clontarf: Norwegians driven from Ireland.

1030 Battle of Stiklestad: death of St Olav.

1066 Battle of Stamford Bridge: Norwegians driven out of England.

1152 Nicholas Breakspeare visits Norway.

1217 First commercial treaty between Bergen and Britain.

1349 The Black Death.

1387 End of old Norwegian dynasty.

1536 Lutheran Reformation.
Norway loses her national government.

1720 End of the Great Northern War with Sweden.

1811 University of Oslo established.

1814 January 14. Treaty of Kiel ends union with Denmark.
May 17. Constitution adopted.
November 4. Union with Sweden established.

1825 *Restorationen* sails for New York.

# Norway

1851    First railway.

1895    Nansen sails from Vardø.

1905    June 7. Union with Sweden dissolved.
        November 18. Prince Carl of Denmark elected King of
        Norway.
        Norwegian whalers in Antarctic.

1909    Christiania–Bergen railway completed.

1911    December 15. Amundsen reaches South Pole.

1925    January 1. Christiania reverts to its old name, Oslo.
        February 9. Norway given sovereignty over Spitz-
        bergen.

1928    First Labour Government.

1940    April 9. German invasion of Norway.
        June 7. King Håkon leaves Tromsø for England.

1945    June 7. King Håkon returns.

1962    Railway to Bodø completed.

1965    Labour Government replaced by a Coalition.

# APPENDIX III
# NORWEGIAN KINGS

## A. Kings of Norway circa 900–1380

| | | |
|---|---|---|
| Harald Fairhair (Harald I) | circa | 900–940 |
| Eric Bloodaxe (Eric I) | „ | 940–945 |
| Håkon the Good (Håkon I) | „ | 945–960 |
| Harald Graypelt (Harald II) | „ | 960–970 |
| Earl Håkon | „ | 970–995 |
| Olav Tryggvesson (Olav I) | | 995–1000 |
| Earls Eric and Svein | | 1000–1016 |
| Olav Haraldsson (St Olav, Olav II) | | 1016–1030 |
| Knut the Great | | 1030–1035 |
| Magnus the Good (Magnus I) | | 1035–1047 |
| Harald Hardråde (Harald III) | | 1047–1066 |
| Olav Kyrri the Peaceful (Olav III) | | 1066–1093 |
| Magnus Bareleg (Magnus II) | | 1093–1103 |
| Eystein Magnusson (Eystein I) | ⎫ | 1103–1125 |
| Sigurd Magnusson the Crusader (Sigurd I) | ⎭ | 1103–1130 |
| Harald Gilchrist (Harald IV) | ⎫ | 1130–1136 |
| Magnus Sigurdsson the Blind (Magnus III) | ⎭ | 1130–1138 |
| Inge Haraldsson (Inge I) | ⎫ | |
| Sigurd Haraldsson (Sigurd II) | ⎬ | 1136–1161 |
| Eystein Haraldsson (Eystein II) | ⎭ | |
| Inge Haraldsson (Inge I) | ⎫ | |
| Sigurd Haraldsson (Sigurd II) | ⎬ | 1136–1161 |
| Eystein Haraldsson (Eystein II) | ⎭ | |

# Norway

Håkon Sigurdsson (Håkon II) · · · · · · · · · · · · · 1161–1162
Magnus Erlingsson (Magnus IV) · · · · · · · · · · 1163–1184
Sverre Sigurdsson · · · · · · · · · · · · · · · · · · · · · · 1184–1202
Håkon Sverresson (Håkon III) · · · · · · · · · · · · 1202–1204
Inge Bårdsson (Inge II) · · · · · · · · · · · · · · · · · 1204–1217
Håkon Håkonsson (Håkon IV) · · · · · · · · · · · · 1217–1263
Magnus Håkonsson the Lawmender (Håkon V) · · 1263–1280
Eric Magnusson (Erik II) · · · · · · · · · · · · · · · · 1280–1299
Håkon Magnusson (Håkon V) · · · · · · · · · · · · · 1299–1319
Magnus Eriksson (Magnus VI) · · · · · · · · · · · · 1319–1355
Håkon Magnusson (Håkon VI) · · · · · · · · · · · · 1355–1380

### B. Kings of Denmark and Norway, 1380–1814

Olav Håkonsson (Olav IV) · · · · · · · · · · · · · · · 1380–1387
Queen Margaret · · · · · · · · · · · · · · · · · · · · · · · 1387–1412
Erik of Pomerania (Erik III) · · · · · · · · · · · · · 1389–1442
Kristopher of Bavaria · · · · · · · · · · · · · · · · · · 1442–1448
Kristian I · · · · · · · · · · · · · · · · · · · · · · · · · · · 1448–1481
Hans · · · · · · · · · · · · · · · · · · · · · · · · · · · · · · · 1481–1513
Kristian II · · · · · · · · · · · · · · · · · · · · · · · · · · 1513–1523
Frederik I · · · · · · · · · · · · · · · · · · · · · · · · · · · 1523–1533
Kristian III · · · · · · · · · · · · · · · · · · · · · · · · · · 1537–1559
Frederik II · · · · · · · · · · · · · · · · · · · · · · · · · · 1559–1588
Kristian IV · · · · · · · · · · · · · · · · · · · · · · · · · · 1588–1648
Frederik III · · · · · · · · · · · · · · · · · · · · · · · · · 1648–1670
Kristian V · · · · · · · · · · · · · · · · · · · · · · · · · · · 1670–1699
Frederik IV · · · · · · · · · · · · · · · · · · · · · · · · · · 1699–1730

# Norwegian Kings

Kristian VI                                        1730–1746

Frederik V                                         1746–1766

Kristian VII                                       1766–1808

Frederik VI                                        1808–1814

Kristian Frederik, King of Norway 17 May–4 November 1814.


C. *Kings of Sweden and Norway, 1814–1905*

Karl XIII                                          1814–1818

Karl Johan (Bernadotte)                            1818–1844

Oskar I                                            1844–1859

Karl XV                                            1859–1872

Oskar II                                           1872–1905


D. *Kings of Norway since 1905*

Håkon VII                                          1905–1957

Olav V                                             1957–

*A Troll*

# INDEX

For the convenience of English readers the Norwegian Å and Ø are here placed after the letters A and O. In Norwegian dictionaries they come at the end of the alphabet.

217

# Index

# Index

# Index

# Index

# Index

# Index

Olav III, 25
Olav IV, 178, 197
Olav Haraldsson, *see* Olav II
Olav Tryggvesson, *see* Olav I
Oppdal, 80
Oppland, 18, 182
Orkney, 85, 133, 182
Orosius, 132
Os, 176
Oslo, ix, 26, 39–43, 45–6, 50, 53, 55–7, 88, 120, 130, 150, 204–5
  and Akersgate, 168
  and Akershus, 1, 3, 27, 60
  and Akersveien, 3
  and Frogner Park, 6, 10, 24
  and Frognerseteren, 2
  and Gamle Aker, 3
  and Historical Museum, 9
  and Hovedøya, 2–4, 27, 51, 179
  and Karl Johan, 4–5, 7, 10
  and Karl Johansgate, 70
  and Kon-Tiki museum, 7, 44
  and maritime museum, 7, 74, 149, 192
  and Munch museum, 7, 10
  and National Gallery, 7
  and National Museum, 5, 90
  and open-air museum, 185
  and Oslo-Bergen line, 37–8
  and State Church, 98, 168
  and the Storting, 4–5, 18, 120, 129, 168, 181
  and Town Hall, 2, 6, 7, 9, 158, 191
  architecture of, 1–3, 10, 160
  bishopric of, 51
  Cathedral of, 36, 196
  Catholic Bishop of, x
  change of name of, 82–3
  communications with, 25, 54, 62, 64, 73, 87, 101, 108–9, 152, 161, 165, 174, 177–80, 188, 194–5
  customs of, 21–4, 28, 163, 190

events in, 19, 65, 68, 71, 76, 181
  latitude of, 151
  people of, 11–16, 106
  University of, 4, 7, 9, 24
Oslofjord, 108, 194–5
Ostra, 189
Oteren, 136, 154
Otta, 59, 61, 63, 83, 174
Ottadal, 60
Ottar, 132
Ottestad, 47
Oxford, 106
Ørnes, 107
Østerdal, 49, 96, 102, 174, 176–7
Østfold, 187, 194
Øveruman, Lake, 165
Øyeren, Lake, 195

Paget, General, 65–6, 73
Palojoensuu, 136, 139
Paris, 106, 120, 133, 153, 161, 200
Paris, Matthew, 173
Parker, Admiral Hyde, 192
Peerson, Cleng, 36
Perry, Admiral, 193
Pettersen, Magnus, 156–8
Philippe Égalité, 153
Plymouth, 36
Poe, Edgar Allan, 114
Poland, 128
Pontoppidan, Erick, 25, 114
Portugal, 28
Prokopios, 132
Pyraminden, 200
Pyrenees, 57

Quains, 146
Quirini, 114–16
Quisling, 50, 178

Ranafjord, 165
Rande, Audun, 125
Rangvald, Jarl, 75
Rankin, P., 65

# Index

# Index

225

# Index